PERSPECTIVES ON WORK & FUN...

"Fun is Frivolous, we know—unless you want to attract
and keep good employees and customers."

INC. MAGAZINE

"Fun is one of the most important—and underrated—
ingredients in any successful venture."

RICHARD BRANSON

"You've achieved success in your field when you don't know
whether what you're doing is work or play."

WARREN BEATTY

"I never did a day's work in my life. It was all fun."

THOMAS ALVA EDISON

"If you take the team out of teamwork, it's just work. Now who wants that?"

MATTHEW WOODRING STOVER

"He who does not get fun and enjoyment out of every day . . .
needs to reorganize his life."

GEORGE MATTHEW ADAMS

"There is little success where there is little laughter."

ANDREW CARNEGIE

"The human race has only one effective weapon—and that is laughter."

MARK TWAIN

"A good laugh is sunshine in the house!"

WILLIAM MAKEPEACE THACKREY

"If A is a success in life, then A equals x plus y plus z.
Work is x; y is play; and z is keeping your mouth shut."

ALBERT EINSTEIN

"If you like your job, if you have inner peace, along with physical health,
you will have had more success than you could possibly have imagined."

JOHNNY CARSON

"Do not take life too seriously. You will never get out of it alive."

ELBERT HUBBARD

Work Made Fun Gets Done!

Work Made FUN Gets Done!

EASY WAYS TO BOOST ENERGY, MORALE, AND RESULTS

BOB NELSON, Ph.D.   **MARIO TAMAYO**

Berrett–Koehler Publishers, Inc.

Berrett-Koehler Publishers, Inc.
1333 Broadway, Suite 1000
Oakland, CA 94612-1921
Tel: (510) 817-2277
Fax: (510) 817-2278
www.bkconnection.com

ORDERING INFORMATION
Quantity sales. Special discounts are available on quantity purchases by corporations, associations, and others. For details, contact the "Special Sales Department" at the Berrett-Koehler address above.

Individual sales. Berrett-Koehler publications are available through most bookstores. They can also be ordered directly from Berrett-Koehler: Tel: (800) 929-2929; Fax: (802) 864-7626; www.bkconnection.com.

Orders for college textbook/course adoption use. Please contact Berrett-Koehler: Tel: (800) 929-2929; Fax: (802) 864-7626.

Distributed to the U.S. trade and internationally by Penguin Random House Publisher Services.

Berrett-Koehler and the BK logo are registered trademarks of Berrett-Koehler Publishers, Inc.

Printed in the United States of America

Berrett-Koehler books are printed on long-lasting acid-free paper. When it is available, we choose paper that has been manufactured by environmentally responsible processes. These may include using trees grown in sustainable forests, incorporating recycled paper, minimizing chlorine in bleaching, or recycling the energy produced at the paper mill.

Cataloging-in-Publication Data is available at the Library of Congress.
Library of Congress Control Number: 2021930308
ISBN: 978-1-5230-9235-2

FIRST EDITION

27 26 25 24 23 22 21 | 10 9 8 7 6 5 4 3 2 1

Book producer: BookMatters; copyeditor: Lou Doucette; proofreader: Janet Reed Blake; cover and text designer: Kim Scott, Bumpy Design

To my loving son,
Geoffrey David Tamayo,
who had a lot of fun in his short life
devoted to helping others

Contents

Preface   ix

Introduction: The Era of Workplace Fun   1

PART I   INDIVIDUAL-ORIENTED FUN   11

Chapter 1: Making Your Own Work Fun   13

Chapter 2: Surprises, Morale Boosters & Thoughtful Gestures   31

PART II   LEADER-ORIENTED FUN   41

Chapter 3: Management Techniques   43

Chapter 4: Meetings & Office Communication   55

Chapter 5: Recognition   67

PART III   TEAM-ORIENTED FUN   79

Chapter 6: Virtual Work   81

Chapter 7: Games, Contests & Competitions   99

Chapter 8: Team Building, Teams & Committees   116

PART IV   ORGANIZATION-ORIENTED FUN   131

Chapter 9: Working Conditions   133

Chapter 10: Office Space & Design   147

Chapter 11: Food   155

Chapter 12: Dogs & Pets   163

Chapter 13: The Arts   170

Chapter 14: Celebrations, Birthdays & Anniversaries   177

Chapter 15: Charities & Volunteering   192

Conclusion & Discussion Guide   201

Acknowledgments   205

Featured Companies   207

About the Authors   219

Preface

People rarely succeed unless they have fun in what they are doing.
—DALE CARNEGIE

This book is for anyone who wants to have more fun at work. This pertains to your own work and the tasks and responsibilities that make up your job—especially boring, rote tasks or large, challenging projects that we often procrastinate about. It also pertains to the work of your immediate team or department members you work with most closely and most often—as well as the broader culture in which your organization operates.

Work made more fun is universally easier and more enjoyable to complete—*and* results in better performance.

We've often heard "Work is serious business. No company would hire someone just to have fun." Of course they wouldn't. But if we can show that having more fun at work helps to get work done, improves relationships and morale, and better achieves desired results, who would object?

"Work" and "fun" have historically been considered polar opposites of each other—it was thought that you could work or you could have fun, but you couldn't do both at the same time—or in the same place. Work is what you do for your paycheck, and fun is what you do on the weekend. Most of us must work to earn money to live, and sometimes enjoying the work we do seems like a luxury we can't afford. Or can we?

For individuals, time at work goes by faster as they become more excited about their work, who they work with, and what they are achieving, which all affect the pride they have in their work, themselves, and the company. The benefits to companies are also substantial, as promoting a fun work environment helps them become an "Employer of Choice," which makes it easier to attract high-performing talent because such talent better enjoy their work and, as a result, stay with the organization longer.

Each year, the Great Place to Work Institute asks thousands of employees to rate their experience of workplace factors, including "This is a fun place to work." On *Fortune*'s "100 Best Companies to Work For" list, employees in companies that are ranked as "great" responded overwhelmingly—an average of 81 percent—that they are working in a "fun" environment. The big takeaway: *Employees at the best companies are having the most fun.* In other words, high performers are having the most fun. And people who are having fun tend to be high performers. It's two sides of the same coin.

At the "good" companies—those that apply for inclusion but do not make the top 100—only 62 percent of employees say they are having fun. That gap in experience between the great and good companies is, surprisingly, one of the largest in the survey.

> "Do not take life too seriously. You will never get out of it alive."
>
> —ELBERT HUBBARD

This is compelling data that supports the notion that any company should strive to make work more fun for employees in their organization.

So why don't more people have fun at work? Is it our puritan work ethic that makes us feel guilty if we are having fun? Is it our fear of being judged, ridiculed, or chastised by others—especially our boss? Do we inherently feel that doing fun things is "wasting time" when we could be, and are being paid to be, productive? Maybe we each harbor a little of all those concerns.

The reasons we don't have more fun at work are many. But we all do have a choice in the matter.

No matter the reason why you're not having as much fun at work as you'd like, this book will show you how to address those concerns and to make fun a natural and ongoing part of how you work going forward. That's what this book offers to individuals, teams, and companies alike: a collection of simple, easy-to-use, real-life examples, techniques, strategies, and best practices to make work more fun—for any worker in any location, on-site or remotely—so work is easier to get done.

> "Fun is Frivolous, we know—unless you want to attract and keep good employees and customers."
>
> —*INC.* MAGAZINE

We will address things you can do to turn any task—be it repetitive, mundane, or even boring—into something that's a little easier to do because you have fun with it. For example, this includes making a game out of the task by challenging yourself to complete it within a certain amount of time, or planning some form of reward for yourself when the task is successfully completed. And the more you do it, the more fun at work starts to snowball. Having fun at one task or responsibility will spill over into other tasks and responsibilities that make them more fun. It will also positively affect those around you so that they better enjoy working with you and come to want more fun at work as well.

You might be wondering, "What if I have a boss who's not very fun?" Well, you can still strive to make your own work fun, but you can also be the person who helps to interject fun into the work environment for others to enjoy, and maybe work on getting your boss to want more fun too!

Of course it's easier to have fun at work if you work for a fun company or at least have a fun manager. We will give examples of what such companies and managers regularly do to create a fun working environment and how you can nudge your manager or others at your company in the "fun" direction. And if you're a manager or CEO or work in human resources, you can make fun happen a lot faster—and ideally on an ongoing basis!

With a different perspective and approach, you can just as easily choose to make work fun, get better at doing so, and help create a fun work environment for yourself and others you work with. As a result, you'll find that you'll tend to enjoy your work more, excel at it more easily, and complete it faster, and you'll be more likely to advance in your career.

You'll also find that fun work is contagious—others will want to join in working with you and maybe just take a little of that positive energy and excitement back with them to their own job and work. That's our expectation for you, and that's why we wrote this book.

Let the fun begin!

Bob Nelson
www.drbobnelson.com
Mario Tamayo
www.tamayogroup.com
San Diego, California

p.s.: If you have an example of fun at work you'd like to share for possible inclusion in a future edition of this book, please send it to us at bob@drbobnelson.com or mario@tamayogroup.com. If you'd like to find out more about any example used in this book, contact us for that as well. Many thanks!

Work Made Fun Gets Done!

INTRODUCTION

The Era of Workplace Fun

Most people chase success at work, thinking that will make them happy.
The truth is that happiness at work will make you successful.

—ALEXANDER KJERULF

Work has historically been oriented just on the activity of working, that is, the tasks and responsibilities we were hired to perform. If we did those tasks and responsibilities as expected, we were paid. If we did our work well over time, we got paid more. And if we did good work for long enough, perhaps we got promoted. Over our career we made more money and were able to support our families, buy houses, and live comfortably. We had security, prestige, and influence. Life was good! If we wanted to have fun in life, we focused those efforts in our personal lives on weekends pursuing hobbies and interests with our family, friends, and other like-minded people.

As time went on, we came to expect more from work. After all, we spend the bulk of our waking hours at work, so maybe we should get more than just a paycheck there? Benefits expanded to include healthcare, vacation, and daycare. We came to socialize with fellow workers outside of working hours.

In more recent years, expectations for work and employers have further expanded. The Millennial generation—currently the largest generation in the workplace—has brought greater expectations for their jobs and their employers. And high on their list of priorities is *fun*. According to a report by Future Workplace, 39 percent of human resource professionals rate Millennials as "fun loving," surpassed only by "tech savvy," which was ranked as the top Millennial attribute by 86 percent of respondents in the survey.

But what is meant by fun at work? One definition given in a research report by **Deloitte Consulting** states that a fun work environment "intentionally encourages, initiates, and supports a variety of enjoyable and pleasurable activities that positively impact the attitude and productivity of the individuals and groups." This is much more than having a Ping-Pong table in the employee break room, free soda in the refrigerator, and an occasional office party. It's about "truly embedding a climate of fun. Building meaningful work in a nurturing environment, filled with growth opportunities underpinned by supportive management and trusted leadership—increasingly a must-have for organizations that want to thrive."

> "Fun is one of the most important—and underrated—ingredients in any successful venture."
> —RICHARD BRANSON

The authors of that research report describe workplaces as now being "amplified social enterprises" and go so far as to say, "Workplace fun is becoming a form of competitive advantage." They labeled the 2020s as the "Era of Workplace Fun."

WHY WE WROTE THIS BOOK

We wrote this book to address the growing expectation people have for their work to be fun. We wanted to take the concept out of the realm of being a soft and fuzzy notion that's rarely discussed and to specifically show how any employee, manager, team, or organization can systematically make fun a part of their individual and team work, as well as a part of their organizational culture. And we wanted to share our own fun experiences at work because fun is integral to who we are as people.

Mario and Bob first met at a week-long company retreat held at Walt Disney World in Orlando, Florida. We both had just started working for The Ken Blanchard Companies, whose founder, Dr. Ken Blanchard, was the co-author of the multimillion-copy best-selling book *The One Minute Manager*. Mario was a project manager, reporting to Bob who was vice president of product development. We worked together with a staff of more than a dozen others to develop management training materials such as facilitator guides, participant workbooks, and various support materials such as assessments, training videos, and audiotape programs. It was generally fun work because we made it fun and the department had a lot of fun working together. The fun made our work easier and more enjoyable and built a goodwill among our staff that lessened stress and fears. It also allowed for more open communication, better problem-solving, and creativity, all of which were essential in working together to overcome challenges and constraints of our jobs as well as to more easily resolve problems as those arose.

When mistakes occurred, we took those in stride. In one instance, Mario and his team missed a typo in a published product by relying too heavily on the automated spellchecker function of the software they were using. The word *manager* ended up being spelled "manger" throughout the product that was printed—ending up being a $10,000 mistake. Mario apprehensively brought the error to Bob's attention. Instead of getting mad or upset, Bob said: "Best lesson you'll have all year! I bet you won't make that mistake again!" And he never did.

After working with Bob for a few months, Mario realized he had failed to mention a three-week European vacation he had planned to surprise his wife. He asked Bob if he could take that time off from work, even though he had not accrued enough vacation time. Although company policy dictated otherwise, Bob approved the vacation, citing that "Mario has done a great job, and I'm confident he will continue to do so. I care more about what will keep him motivated than following a policy."

While Mario, a big fan of Elvis Presley, was gone, Bob framed and matted a 6-foot full-length poster of the King that Mario had on his office wall. When Mario returned from vacation, he was surprised and delighted to see the King in a matted frame on his wall. Bob didn't stop there. For years, every time Bob traveled to or through Memphis (Elvis's hometown) for work, he brought back some Elvis memorabilia for Mario.

We constantly did fun things. We brought masseuses and hypnotists into our department, took afternoons off from work to see movies, and even took the team to Disneyland in a limo with a driver who was an Elvis impersonator. We created skits and videos together. One particularly funny video for the new-employee orientation featured our janitor delivering a stand-up comedy routine about the company's values and products.

> "He who does not get fun and enjoyment out of every day . . . needs to reorganize his life."
>
> —GEORGE MATTHEW ADAMS

You might read these antics and think, "Okay for you, but (1) my company isn't going to send me to Disney World, and (2) how did you get any work done??" The answer is: "We earned the right to have fun because we did *great* work—and a lot of it." At one point Bob remembers talking to his counterpart at a major competitor of the company and describing the department's capabilities and production, and that person told him: "If my boss knew what you all are achieving, I'd lose my job!" Performers like to have fun, and they *deserve* to have fun.

Years later the department members honored and roasted Bob by mocking up a book jacket that Bob had supposedly authored entitled *If I'm in Charge Here, Why Is Everybody Laughing?*—complete with funny testimonials and quotes.

After 10 years or so, we both eventually left the Blanchard organization for other pursuits but remained friends and colleagues. Thirty years later, we're still having fun together. Bob's wife, Jennifer, says, "It's amazing they get anything done, because all I ever hear when they're working together is them laughing!" We work hard and we get a lot of work done, but we always have fun in the process!

WHAT OUR PHILOSOPHY IS

Our philosophy of fun at work is that it is possible for any worker to have fun and benefit from having done so. Here are some dos and don'ts to help guide you on your journey:

Do #1: Be playful; choose to have fun. We believe having fun at work is a matter of choice. Take your work seriously, but yourself lightly. If you start with an attitude of fun, you will more than likely find a willing audience in those you work with, which will make fun easier to sustain. As Abraham Lincoln reportedly said, "Most folks are about as happy as they make up their minds to be."

Do #2: Be open & flexible. We know it's easy to have fun at work if you put your mind to it, but you also need to be open to what others you work with feel is fun. If you only take away one thing from this book, remember this: Follow our Fun principle—Make it safe and fun for everyone. What's fun varies widely from person to person, so you have to have some flexibility, acceptance, and encouragement of others' versions of fun.

In her doctoral research on the topic of fun at work, Tiffany McDowell found, for example, that men in white-collar jobs said they had fun at work when "connecting with others," while women in white-collar jobs felt they were having fun at work when "they were doing something they were good at" or "doing creative work." Blue-collar men, however, saw their work as fun when they "enjoyed the job itself" and "when they were able to use their own initiative at work," while blue-collar women saw their jobs as "fun when they felt they were really accomplishing something of value with their work." And the different views of fun among employees also vary by age, personality, nationality, and many other factors. What's fun to some may not be fun to others, so you need to get to know those you work with and allow them the freedom and flexibility to have fun in ways they appreciate.

Do #3: Experiment; try new things. Part of what makes something fun (and funny) is the element of surprise, its freshness, and creativity.

Think outside of the proverbial box as to what could be done differently. Ask, "What do others expect in this situation?" and then do the opposite or at least something different from what has always been done in the past.

Do #4: Learn, refine & reapply. No matter what you attempt as a way to have fun, you can learn from it. What worked and what didn't? If you did it again, what would you change or improve upon? Just as telling a joke well takes practice, timing, and nuance, so does any other attempt at fun and humor! The more you work at it, the better you and your coworkers will become at having fun while still getting your work done.

Do #5: Be patient. If others you work with don't readily accept your idea of fun or don't participate—hang in there! Invite and encourage their ideas for fun things to do at work. Seek a supporter above you in the organization, perhaps your manager or even someone higher who seems to have a "fun" personality and appreciates the topic.

And as for the don'ts, these are the mirror opposites of the dos:

Don't #1: Don't force fun on others. Fun has to be safe; it can't be forced on others. No one should be made to participate in an activity deemed "fun" by others if they don't want to. As Wai Poc, an executive coach in San Francisco, California, puts it: "Forced fun is not fun. Fun is what fits you and your work environment. It always bothered me when a company I worked for did a 'fun activity.' I always felt like, 'Great, so this is supposed to be fun, and yet I felt forced to put on a happy face.'" You can't force fun on anyone, but instead allow them to participate as they are comfortable—and support them in the process. How do you ensure people feel comfortable and experience fun? Get to know them and learn what they enjoy, and encourage them to do more of those things.

Don't #2: Don't be rigid and predictable. Don't dictate what is fun or when it can occur at work. Don't impose rules on others about fun. Don't become the fun police; don't be a killjoy. Allow people to be who they are and do what they prefer to have fun. And don't reprimand or punish people if an attempted "fun" activity falls flat, but rather encourage everyone to learn from the experience and try something different next time. (Or plan to repeat the activity if it worked well!)

Don't #3: Don't keep doing the same things. If variety is the spice of life, then fun is your chance to add some seasoning! Grant permission to stretch and try new things. If the group is new to having fun, maybe run your plans by the boss first. There's no guarantee that all— or any—of your ideas will work, but if you have fun in the process, that's half the battle won!

Don't #4: Don't overlook learning from fun things you've tried. To get better at anything, you have to debrief what was done, what went well, and what could be improved. So is the case with fun at work. Take time to consider what you did and how you could make it even better the next time.

> "If you take the team out of teamwork, it's just work. Now who wants that?"
>
> —**MATTHEW WOODRING STOVER**

Don't #5: Don't give up. The more fun you attempt, the easier it will be for others to join in, and at some point fun will become a part of your work culture that everyone will come to appreciate and expect! In our experience, having fun is contagious and others will want to participate, contribute as they deem appropriate, and eventually take the lead in having even more fun.

HOW THIS BOOK IS SET UP

This book is organized into four sections to focus on examples of fun at four levels: individual, leader, team, and organization.

Individual-Oriented Fun. The first section of the book focuses on having fun in your own work, which is the starting point for the topic. Until you can make your own daily tasks enjoyable, you'll never be able to have fun in working with others or in a group.

Leader-Oriented Fun. The second section of the book looks at what any manager or leader can do to instill fun in the work of those they manage. More than anyone else, managers set the tone at work, so it's important for them to lead the charge in having the group's work be fun and the act of working together be fun.

Team-Oriented Fun. The third section of the book examines all the fun things you can do as part of a team or work group, which is substantial! Again, if you bring the right attitude of fun to the work group, and look for opportunities to insert fun, you'll make inroads into the group attitude and practice of having more fun in working together.

Organization-Oriented Fun. The fourth and largest section of this book covers a multitude of activities, events, and strategies that can be used in any organization to encourage—and legitimize—having more fun at work. The more that fun can become sanctioned through practices, policies, and tradition, the more likely it will become a part of your organization's culture, that is, "how we do things around here."

HOW TO CREATE A FUN WORK CULTURE

All organizations are made up of individuals, so the most basic change happens at that level. But a culture of fun can't be maintained or thrive without the support of your manager and higher-ups in the organization. To ultimately have fun be an integral part of your organization's work culture, individuals need to have (1) an awareness of the importance of fun, (2) opportunities to have or insert fun into their work, and (3) a supportive environment that encourages fun. As the organization and its leadership systematically encourage more fun practices and activities—and ideally actively participate themselves—a change will take place over time so that fun becomes part of the organization's culture, that is, one of the expected norms of the organization and all its members as to "how we do things around here."

> "If you like your job, if you have inner peace, along with physical health, you will have had more success than you could possibly have imagined."
>
> —JOHNNY CARSON

If you are a leader without a title, you can do things in your work group and recruit other fun people to start a "grassroots" movement.

It takes longer, but you can build momentum for change. If you are a supervisor or manager, you'll have a more significant impact on your work group. And if you work in human resources or are a director or above, you have a larger sphere of influence, so your impact can be broader and you can help your organization change even more quickly. Lead with your own fun behaviors and give others implicit permission to do the same. The ideas and examples that follow in this book will give you insight into what others have successfully done, and what you can do as well!

HOW TO BEST USE THIS BOOK

This book is meant to be a resource for ongoing reference for ideas to try and learnings to cement for your own purposes. It can be accessed when you are looking to do something new and different, or passed around your team for others to select ideas they'd like to try for themselves individually and as a group. It can even be slipped to the one person who doesn't "get it" and is still operating out of a framework and expectations of a former work era long past that feels there is no place for fun in a serious business. Any way you use it, we know this book will provide an ongoing source of possibilities for you, your team, and your organization.

We can each choose to make work fun, just as we can choose to be miserable at work (or by default, become miserable by not making a choice to be otherwise) and, in the process, make those around us miserable as well—even those at home. (Note: Research shows the average person spends 15 percent of their time at home complaining about their boss!)

We hope you choose wisely and have as much fun as possible in the process!

 **WARNING**

- The examples and ideas in the chapters you are about to read are true.

- Should you decide to try one or more of the examples, you do so at the risk of complete fun and enjoyment, for yourself and for others you work with and for.

- No animals were harmed in the planning and implementing of these activities.

 **REMEMBER**

- What's fun for some may not be for others.

- Know thy people well.

- Keep it safe and fun for everyone!

PART I
Individual-Oriented Fun

Fun at work starts with every individual, initially in how they think about the topic and then in how they apply fun to their everyday work tasks, responsibilities, and interactions with others at work.

If you want your work to be more fun, *you* need to make that a priority and have a playful, fun-oriented attitude about the topic, look for opportunities, and seek to embed fun in different ways in your daily work activities. By taking responsibility for your own fun at work, you will quickly attract and encourage other like-minded coworkers, which will make it easier to have even more fun!

We believe that any work assignment can be made fun if you put your mind to it. We'll share personal strategies we and others have for getting through the rote, repetitive, or boring parts of our jobs, and ways you can learn to do the same.

Any change starts with some self-reflection followed by some "baby steps" in trying new behaviors, determining what worked and learning from what didn't, and then reapplying your efforts accordingly.

The chapters in this section are "Making Your Own Work Fun" and "Surprises, Morale Boosters & Thoughtful Gestures."

CHAPTER 1

Making Your Own Work Fun

I just go to the office to enjoy myself; work automatically happens.

—JITENDRA ATTRA

Work made fun starts in every job with every individual worker. According to recent research reported by *Business News Daily*, while fun could be considered a distraction, it actually has the ability to improve employee resilience and optimism, which leads to better attention to tasks. When we make a task fun, we tend to be more eager to dig in and complete it, as opposed to having it be a dreaded activity that we put off doing—maybe even multiple times.

When Bob has a work task or project that for some reason he is dreading, he likes to talk it through with someone—a colleague, a friend, or his wife—to warm up to the task. Often this helps him understand exactly what he's dreading about the task, and the fear of the unknown evaporates as the task or project is examined. If the work is something he hasn't done before, talking about it leads to various options that can then be weighed against one another, prioritized, and—suddenly—he's into the work activity and gets into a flow. If it's a mundane task, like organizing his desk or balancing his checkbook, he does the activity as a break from a larger project he's working on. In either large or small tasks, Bob has fun making progress on things he's trying to achieve. And when someone shares something fun with him—a funny text message, internet meme, funny story, or joke—he makes a point to share that with at least three other people, reliving the humor each time he shares it with someone else.

When Mario is faced with a boring work task to do, he likes to think of the big "why and win" in doing the task. If it's a big task, he'll break it up to make it more manageable. Plus he finds ways to reward himself for progress he makes—perhaps taking a break or having a candy bar. If the task takes some discipline, he'll get up early and focus on "knocking it out." He also has kept a gratitude log for years, which helps to keep him constantly focused on the positives in his life.

These are just a few of the approaches that we, Bob and Mario, use to make our work more fun. In this chapter we will explore techniques and strategies that have worked for many others and could likely work for you as well. In fact, we were surprised at the extensive range of approaches that people use to make their work fun! It almost seemed that no two people had the same approach to the topic, and it's encouraging to know there's no limit to the ways to bring joy to your work.

The more you expand your own strategies for making work fun, the more fun will become a standard approach for getting your work done and the more fun you'll have. This is important because until you embrace having fun yourself at whatever tasks or job you are doing, you'll never develop a broader appreciation for the topic.

LEARN TO EMBRACE FUN

A former professor and CEO of several companies, Brad Zehner, Ph.D., located near Austin, Texas, shares his philosophy on fun at work: "Once I earned an MBA, my promise to myself was straightforward, 'I will never do a job unless it is fun at least 70 percent of the time.' As the eldest of 14 children, I did every manual labor job there is to earn money to pay for university. Consequently, I was one of the strange individuals who loved the creative challenges of solving management problems of all types. I was never bored."

Ramon Grijalva, Ph.D., vice chair of the **Institute of Electrical and Electronic Engineers** (IEEE), based in Hollywood, California, says, "So much of life is playing a game with oneself! When I worked with Long Beach [California] government they had forms for everything and it was boring and painful to have to complete those, so I would mentally 'suit up' and go into 'mechanical mode' to talk myself into the right frame of mind. I'd work around the periphery to set up the work (getting organized, creating an invoice, etc.) and then dig in to the dreaded task to complete it as quickly as possible."

> "You must have discipline to have fun."
>
> —JULIA CHILD

"I think the biggest overarching approach that keeps me engaged and having fun at work is choosing to have a mission-driven career and life," says Jessica Sims, MD, an emergency medicine specialist in Los Angeles, California. "My career mission is to do the things I am able to drive healthcare towards a more reliable, equitable and sustainable industry. My life 'mission' is to leave every person and place I interact with happier and better.

"On a day-to-day basis and also during more profound career moments I try to measure my big *and* small choices against these missions. Even when I find the task at hand falls outside my standard duties or well 'beneath' my abilities and qualifications, if it satisfies these missions I still find satisfaction in that work. For example, sometimes I may find myself doing secretarial or nurse work to help a patient. I'm not okay with ignoring the need because 'that's not my job,' although it might also be frustrating to do someone else's work especially with my own duties, two advanced degrees and 25 years of professional experience.

"When I realize that these small tasks make a difference and also shows the staff that those things matter, I find it more meaningful than the tasks themselves might be. I also think about a couple of Martin Luther King quotes: 'It's never the wrong time to do the right thing' and 'If I can't do great things I'll do small things in a great way.'"

Charlie Chase, president of **Genetic Synergy** in Steamboat Springs, Colorado, says: "What is fun varies widely from person to person, for example, one person might like to sing or hear music, someone else might get excited about efficiency, while another person is happiest being left alone to work on a project."

Fun Things to Do on a 5- to 10-Minute Break

1. Praise someone for something specific.
2. Do something nice for someone else.
3. Look at a favorite app.
4. Tell someone a joke.
5. Meditate.
6. Listen to a favorite song or two.
7. Stretch your large muscle groups.
8. Go for a quick walk outside.
9. Walk up a flight of stairs.
10. Donate to a favorite charity.

What's fun for him? Sitting down at the computer and devising an investment strategy: "When you're happy, you're more creative and it spills over into all aspects of your life."

Charlie recommends using ColorCode.com (a 20-minute color code test on the internet) to determine your innate motivation, which involves four colors:

- **Reds:** Need to look good technically, be right, and be respected. They are strong leaders and love challenges.

- **Blues:** Need to have integrity and be appreciated. They are focused on quality and creating strong relationships.

- **Whites:** Need to be accepted and treated with kindness. They are logical, objective, and tolerant of others.

- **Yellows:** Need to be noticed and have fun. They love life, social connections, and being positive and spontaneous.

"You can diagnose others via their words, energy, and timeframe: (1) if they're more introverted or extroverted, and (2) if they're more logical or emotional. How you communicate with others is essential: each color preference communicates differently, but everyone can learn to speak everyone else's preferred language."

> "You've achieved success in your field when you don't know whether what you're doing is work or play."
>
> —**WARREN BEATTY**

IT'S THE LITTLE THINGS

Feeling overwhelmed? Katie Sheehan, the marketing manager of Oakland, California–based **Berrett-Koehler Publishers**, changed her mental outlook when she changed the title of her to-do list to a "fun list."

Sue Burch, senior learning specialist at **Insight Enterprises** in Sugar Grove, Illinois, says: "Technology is great; however, crumpling paper is more satisfying than deleting. So I often put challenging work on Post-it notes so that I can then destroy the note and throw it in the trash when tasks are complete. If you have a white board, this is a great place for the notes to live."

"The secret to my having more fun at work is to have those precious little ear buds in and some good jazz music playing. It's common now for managers to allow (even encourage) such activity. They quickly reap the rewards as employees are grateful, engaged and more likely to stick around for a while longer!" says Sharon Jordan-Evans, president, **Jordan Evans Group**, and co-author of multiple books, including *Love 'Em or Lose 'Em: Getting Good People to Stay.*

Paola Arango, who works for a consulting firm in Colombia, South America, says, "I wear my hair and dress happily. I use an image consultant to guide me in the colors and aspects that make me look and feel better: They connect me with my style, essence and joy. Dressing up and putting on makeup for work is most days my harbinger that it will be a day with lots of potential. I can wear a different ring, a perfume, an eye shadow, a lipstick or my fun shoes. I also try to imagine that the company I work for is my company and that is why I do my best."

Donna Fremed, human resources consultant business partner for **DLF Global** in San Diego, California, says she makes work, personal tasks, or projects fun by "choosing the pen, colored marker or pencil I use before starting to work. Some of the pens have memories of where I got them from. For example, I have a Coca-Cola pen from a business trip to Atlanta. Also, I have a new 'fineline' set of markers that I will use to draw and write. I can't wait to start drawing with them!"

> "As usual, the serious me is working hard, but the real me is having fun."
>
> —JOHN REED

"I use colorful markers and a notepad to take notes, draw pictures for notes, etc. especially when on conference calls," says Christine Gilmore, vice president of training for **Bell Partners** in Greensboro, North Carolina. "One of my office mates has a box of funny things on her desk, so she will hold up a funny cut-out monster on the video phone, you look away and look back and there he is; she will walk into a brainstorming meeting with a purple mohawk wig, just anything from the box to catch you off guard whether you are in person, on Zoom or a conference call. We leave little plastic ninja characters on people's desks with a note that says I caught you doing something awesome. We will break out in a glow stick dance party on a team Zoom or in a team meeting. (One must always have glow sticks in their desk!) We start each team meeting with an icebreaker, we rotate who is responsible for coming up with it and leading it each week. Right now with everyone working from home, every once in a while I send care packages to my team with some of their favorite things."

At the **Administrative Office of the Courts** in Wilmington, Delaware, trainer/educator Allison Gallo lightens her and her colleagues' days by making faces at them through their open office doors while walking down the halls. She also keeps toys in her office—stress balls, Slinkys, a rubber chicken, light-up toys, a pair of doll hands. "They're in a spot where we all can easily reach them." And she isn't afraid to use fun in ways to help get her work done. Allison once had an extraordinarily hard time getting a report she needed from a colleague. She had a creative idea. She asked a team member to take a photo of her holding a stuffed bunny rabbit by the ears with one hand while holding a hair dryer to its head with the other. She printed the picture and pasted letters cut from magazines around it to spell out the message "Send me the 'X' report, or the bunny gets it!" Says Gallo: "My novel approach to problem-solving made everyone laugh."

> "Laugh as much as possible, always laugh. It's the sweetest thing one can do for oneself and one's fellow human beings."
>
> **—MAYA ANGELOU**

Donna R. Monroe, assistant to the chief at the **Pocatello Police Department** in Pocatello, Idaho, also brings in the little toys from bubble gum machines, McDonald's, The Dollar Store, and little Nerf toys like basketball hoops, 3D glasses, Pez candies and shooters, and so on to work. She has a small collection in a box and pulls them out occasionally for playtime! It allows her and others around her to be kids again. It's fun. She also gives nicknames to nearly everyone she works with. She uses whatever comes to mind (that's appropriate, and nice, of course) and calls people by those names. They reciprocate, so she has quite a few nicknames herself as a result. That's also fun.

"We all know what it feels like to be running on empty or at least running on fumes and pushing to the max just to get it done," says author and leadership coach Patty Vogan. "Our cars have warning lights and sounds that tell us low fuel, low tire pressure, open door, or electrical problem. You don't miss those, do you?"

Vogan, who also chairs CEO peer groups for **Vistage International**, offers two main strategies to unlock your energy and increase your fun so you can "refuel" before you are running on fumes. Or worse, running on empty:

Strategy #1: Drink Water. "Your brain is between 65 percent and 85 percent water; in fact, so are your kidneys and liver," says Vogan. "Do you feel your brain, kidneys and liver working? No. When do you feel them? When they *stop working*. A multiple of symptoms occur with dehydration. The magical pill for more energy under the physical category is to drink water. A rule of thumb to start with: Take half of your body weight and turn it into ounces and that is the amount for you to drink daily. If you want to prevent a heart attack or stroke, according to the Mayo Clinic, drink one glass of water before bed and before taking a bath. Also, staying hydrated during the day helps to stave off night-time leg cramps. Drink the right amount of water daily for your body. The bonus is your skin will look better too."

Fun Things to Do on a 30- to 90-Minute Break

1. Go outside and get some fresh air.
2. Walk in the park.
3. Listen to a TED talk.
4. Read/listen to a book on tape.
5. Use the company fitness facilities.
6. Ride a bike to/from work.
7. Learn a new skill.
8. Play a team game.
9. Visit a local museum.
10. Go shopping.

Strategy #2: Be Spiritual. "When it comes to spirituality our job is simple, but *we* make it difficult," says Vogan. "It's three simple words. Love one another. Our job is to show, demonstrate and act out love to one another. I was *not* put on this planet to be self-centered, take up space and then die. I do not believe you were either."

Vogan says we all have gifts and talents that are to be shared. Take your talents and make them useful by serving others. "Slow your pace to win the race by serving others.

"Whenever you talk with people that have just come from doing something in the philanthropic, charitable or serving realm, you will hear them say, 'Wow, I got more out of serving than those we served,'" says Vogan. "The key to filling your spiritual energy tank is to serve others.

"In summary, if you want more energy, drink and measure your water intake to refuel your physical energy tank. Plus love one another through service to fill your spiritual energy tank," concludes Vogan.

Five Steps to Start Serving Others:

1. Hold the door open for someone.

2. Give an honest compliment.

3. Take inventory of your talents; offer them anywhere.

4. Listen: Being fully listened to feels so much like being loved people can't tell the difference.

5. Show up and be kind.

—PATTY VOGAN

BREAK IT DOWN

Jeff Toister, an author and instructor for **Toister Performance Solutions Inc**. in San Diego, California, says: "Here's a simple trick I use, which I adapted from the Pomodoro Technique to get work done and make it fun."

1. Choose a specific project to focus on.

2. Turn off all distractions, including phone, email, and other notifications.

3. Set a timer for 20 minutes.

4. Give yourself permission to focus on that task until the timer goes off.

"I often find this gets me into a flow state of deep concentration and enjoyment. The work comes more naturally, and I get more done. Almost inevitably, I'm disappointed when the timer goes off!"

Want a fun way to learn a new software program (or improve your skills on one you already think you know)? Michael Laughlin, curriculum designer, Corporate Contact Center (CCC) for **Centene Corporation** in St. Louis, Missouri, has a suggestion: "Have a small reward ready (cup of favorite beverage, 15-minute well-deserved break, chat with coworker to show the new skill, trick, tip) and set a timer for 30 minutes. Before you start the timer, go to the software manufacturer's website to look at features you did not know existed (or how to start the program if you are beginning) and then go to YouTube to search for that feature in a short video. Open your software, turn on the timer and start the YouTube video. As the tip progresses, do each step by pausing the video and work it out on your own computer/device. Do each step until the task is complete. Now, turn off the video and do it for yourself. Turn off the timer and . . . Celebrate!"

CASE STUDY

MAKING A DULL JOB MORE FUN

Anyone can make their job a little more fun just by trying. Debi Foster, who works for Communications & Government Affairs at the Mission Support and Test Services in North Las Vegas, Nevada, describes how she made a dull job much more fun:

We have a company store that sells company logo items, discount tickets, and gift cards. Employees can purchase items or we have an award program that they get a $25 or $50 certificate to spend in the store.

I work the store for one hour a day and sometimes it is busy and sometimes it is a chore to sit in there, knowing that I have plenty of other things I should be working on at my desk. So to make it more enjoyable to me I try to engage the employees that come to the window with questions or suggestions on the items they are purchasing instead of just taking their money or certificate and moving them on.

When they are redeeming an award I ask them what they did to earn it, some will give a quick answer, some go into detail, and some even say they aren't sure why; but whatever the answer I think they appreciate my interest. This helps me as I also administer the award program and when the employee tells me they don't know why they received it, I can go back to the managers and remind them to be more specific when presenting the awards.

When employees purchase movie tickets, I ask what they plan to see. Or if they purchase tickets to Legoland California, I point out that they should definitely check out the Miniland USA display where they have the Las Vegas strip built out of Legos (and other cities too). Even when they choose a gift card, I encourage them to use it for themselves (since they earned the award) instead of giving it to their spouse or kids. There are some employees that don't engage, just take their stuff and hurry back to work; some that are surprised I am interested; and others that get so engaged they have made me late closing the store!

Freelance writer Carol Patton of Las Vegas, Nevada, says, "When tackling a task I dislike, I break it down into stages and reward myself along the way. For example, if I complete this portion of the task, I can take a walk, call a friend, or eat that Fudgsicle I've been eyeing in the freezer. Other times, I may work Saturday mornings to make the workweek less challenging or hectic. It takes the edge off Monday mornings. I rarely cram all of my tasks into a Monday–Friday, 8–5, routine."

Laurie Donnelly, learning and development specialist for **Retooling the Workforce** based in Los Angeles, California, offers up the following strategies for making work fun:

> "Creativity is intelligence having fun."
> **—ALBERT EINSTEIN**

- Starting with the deadline, I number the tasks and set a duration for completion for each. Goals are set for when each set of tasks needs to be completed by in order to meet the deadline as though they are sales quotas. As I reach a milestone, I give myself a reward. Mani/pedi anyone?

- Yo-Yo Ma played Johann Sebastian Bach's six unaccompanied cello suites in their entirety at a single performance in 2015. He played for nearly three hours by memory with one short intermission. It is inspiring to listen to and watch him perform gracefully despite this daunting task and in front of an audience of 8,000. It seems as though a cosmic force is moving his hands as the majestic sounds reverberate from his cello throughout the hall. As I listen and work, I imagine that, similarly, my hands are influenced by that same force to accentuate the e-learning content that I'm designing. (See Yo-Yo Ma—Bach Six Cello Suites—BBC Proms 2015 on the Internet.)

> "The best advice I ever received came from my mother: 'Do at least one fun thing every day.'"
>
> —CLIFFORD COHE

- When I have a mental block, I "telecommute." Technically, it's called somatic therapy. I like to imagine I'm at Coachella 2019 dancing in the audience to Fisher's "Losing It." Another favorite is to travel back in time to experience Eminem's "Till I Collapse" live in concert. It helps that the music video is from the movie *Real Steel* with Hugh Jackman. Crank it up!

- A silver lining of the pandemic is that I can take a 15-minute break and do yoga stretches (also considered a somatic treatment), paint with watercolors or have a hot, lavender-scented bath all of which rejuvenate my creativity.

- When I'm at the office, I walk over to MOCA (Museum of Contemporary Art in Los Angeles) and envision ways to complete my instructional design work as though it will be a work of art hanging in a museum.

- Likewise, I'll walk to the public library and read a classic text for 10 minutes. Reading the printed page improves comprehension and, for me, inspiration. (See https://hechingerreport.org/evidence-increases-for-reading-on-paper-instead-of-screens/.) If there isn't time, printing out the project and sitting outside to review it will work in a snap.

Dominique Fruchtman, a programs director for **Professionals in Human Resources Association** (PIHRA) in Los Angeles and owner of an escape game in Palm Springs, California, reports that when she was a child, her mother once gave her 35 boxes and said she needed to wrap them all in two hours during the holidays. Instead of complaining or panicking, she created a method: She organized the boxes by size, cut all the paper first, lined up pieces of tape on a yardstick, etc. Many years later she does the same steps when wrapping gifts today. Her strategies for having fun and getting more done model that approach, including:

- Determine a strategy/new approach—which doesn't have to be perfect. Set a timer—have complete focus. See how much you can do—try to best yourself! Like a form of hypnosis—game to better your own technique and speed.

- Break the task down into its logical steps, perhaps in a way it has never been done before. For example, in doing housekeeping, she starts with a bio break, gets a bottle of water, turns the phone off, tells others not to disturb her, then *digs in*.

- Make a game out of it and work always goes faster. For example, if she has to proofread something, she acts like she's in the proofreading Olympics and shoots for the best time ever.

- Make a list, then cross off "make a list" to show progress.

- Call a friend for motivation.

VARY YOUR APPROACH

"When I was a little girl, one of the things my brother and I enjoyed doing was 'spearminting' in the kitchen mixing up concoctions like peanut butter mixed with chocolate," says Veronica S. Harvey, Ph.D., founder and principal of **Schmidt Harvey Consulting LLC** in Phoenix, Arizona. "As adults experimenting can be fun too! Being curious, trying out new things and taking time to create new and better ways to do things can make work a joyful experience. Finding ways to learn is what continues to make work fun for me. As an expert in the area of learning agility I'm passionate about the importance of learning agility to long-term success, but we often overlook how much *joy* learning can bring. It is fun to put together past experiences with new insights to develop a fresh new approach. In the midst of the pandemic, I was completing a book that I was coediting; because I was learning so much from the writings of the other contributors, it felt (most of the time) more like a hobby than a chore. It was inspiring and fun to 'connect the dots.' What made it even more rewarding was to know that the development of learning agility was a topic that could be empowering to many and result in others finding more joy and fun in their own work."

Albert Frazia, chief human resources officer for **DeBragga & Spiller Inc**. in Jersey City, New Jersey, shares an approach he has applied to boost his morale, energy, productivity, and fun in his projects and deliverables: "If I am working on a particularly challenging task or project, I will sometimes go 'off-site' to work or think it through. A favorite location

> "Have fun, even if it's not the same kind of fun everyone else is having."
>
> —C. S. LEWIS

for me was Bryant Park in midtown Manhattan (when I worked in Manhattan). In the spring and summer, chairs and tables are set out on the lawn for use by visitors. Bryant Park offers a balance of the relaxation of a natural park surrounded by the excitement of Manhattan. I found this temporary re-location restorative and quite an enhancement to my productivity."

Hoodsa Ghazvinian, management consultant/leadership development advisor at the **Industrial Management Institute** in Iran, uses two personal habits to remove pressure from work and make it fun:

> "Laughter is an instant vacation."
>
> —**MILTON BERLE**

Habit 1: I watch 1–2 best concerts of my favorite singers. Singers are great screen players and they share fun and energy with audiences. I tune myself with that energy and I think I am entertaining others while being my best version. And then everything becomes like a screenplay; I'm full of courage, energy and happiness.

Habit 2: I paint any idea I have first. When the idea is expressed on paper in a colorful way, I find it easier to make the idea happen in reality.

Steve Donahue, best-selling author of *Shifting Sands*, located in Victoria, British Columbia, says, "Here's something fun that I do when I deliver a speech: I often tell a story about my journey across the Sahara Desert during my keynote presentations. The story is woven throughout the speech and the audience soon becomes familiar with this unique storytelling technique I employ where I play an African drum as the automated slide show advances through the

> "The trouble with life in the fast lane is you get to the other end in an awful hurry."
>
> —JOHN JENSEN

photos. To mix things up I give my clicker to a random person in the audience and he or she must decide when to go to the next slide based solely on the story I'm narrating. Of course they *never* get it right. They're too fast or too slow, which forces me to adjust and adlib much to the delight of the rest of the audience. It's fun for me as well because, let's face it, I know how the story is going to end. I've told that story a thousand times. This brings excitement into something that is a familiar, even routine, part of my work."

CHAPTER 2

Surprises, Morale Boosters & Thoughtful Gestures

All I want to do is have some fun.
I get the feeling, I'm not the only one.

—SHERYL CROW

What does it take to allow employees to have more fun in their work? Happy employees make for more productive employees. University of Warwick conducted a study of more than 700 participants, which concluded that increased happiness led to a 12 percent spike in productivity, and according to research by Ben Waber, companies can increase productivity by up to 25 percent by making small changes at work that increase employees' sense of fun and satisfaction, such as overlapping lunch breaks and the placement of coffee stations. So it's worth the time it takes to help spread a little joy in the workplace, whether it's for one other person or your entire work group. Following are some simple but fun things others have done in the workplace. Have it be a "starter set" for creating your own toolbox of fun things to try with others you work with!

8 Recognition Tips to Boost Morale

1. Give genuine thank-yous in person, by handwritten note, email, or social app.

2. Give full attention and make eye contact when you praise them.

3. Have a spontaneous celebration.

4. Announce employee accomplishments to the entire company.

5. Make up categories to award deserving employees.

6. Make a hand- or custom-made Fun awards from recycled materials.

7. Install and use team shout-outs boards.

8. Give gift cards—for things *they* really value.

When colleagues are under tight deadlines or high-pressure projects, Jill Boone, assistant VP of European talent for **Enterprise Holdings** of Surrey, United Kingdom, emails inspirational quotes to them Monday mornings—sometimes daily. "I know they're getting lots of other emails with tasks to do, so at least one of them is just to offer inspiration and motivation," says Boone.

"There's nothing quite like a sticky note," says author Kelly Epperson. She uses the notes in two ways. One, she writes quotes, silly sayings, and inside jokes and posts them throughout her office. Sometimes, she puts them on computer screens saying things like, "Damn, you look good." Two, she walks around her office with a note on her forehead that says, "I'm having a bad day!" "Just having it on immediately improves everyone's mood. Try it!" says Epperson.

"The most successful mood-enhancing technique I had as a manager of graphic artists," says Rebecca Taft of **PacBell**, "was to use stickers when I approved something they had put together." Forgoing the usual "Great job!" types or ones used in grade schools, Taft gave seasonal stickers. These included little snowmen, Santas, or wreaths at Christmas; flags and fireworks for Independence Day; black cats or jack-o'-lanterns at Halloween; and so on. "It was corny, but people really enjoyed them. Many peeled them off and kept them on their monitors. I kept a large supply on hand so people didn't always receive the same ones," adds Taft.

Donna Gintz, an instructional designer in the Phoenix, Arizona, office of the **Department of Economic Security**, uses the Blue Mountain app to send online greeting cards for any occasion to colleagues. She also creates videos and inserts funny images.

Everyone loves jokes. A member of the advertising department of **Business First** in Louisville, Kentucky, encouraged her department to broadcast daily jokes, motivational messages, success stories—anything to help people most enjoy their work.

Employees tried to make each other laugh at the **Bank of America** offices in San Francisco during its Laugh-a-Day Challenge, which they held for one month. Each employee tried to make coworkers laugh with cartoons and jokes. Winners received T-shirts and books that showcase the best jokes and cartoons.

On their own, a few employees at **LaSalle**, the Chicago, Illinois—headquartered global real estate investment firm, encouraged their colleagues by "chalking the walk." They visited the homes of coworkers living nearby and wrote positive messages on the sidewalks with colored chalk.

Donna Monroe, the assistant to the chief at the **Pocatello (Idaho) Police Department** is also the force's popcorn chef. Monroe brings a popcorn maker to work on officially named "popcorn days." She brings along paper theater bags, flavoring salts, and butter, which she melts in the microwave as the corn pops. "Everyone smells it, and they all start

> ### 4 Steps to Telling Great Jokes
>
> 1. Set the context.
> 2. Only give information that's necessary. Less is more.
> 3. Pause, then deliver "unexpected" punch line.
> 4. Never told a joke in public? Practice it first!

gathering! Lots of smiles and thank-yous," says Monroe. Some workers contribute to buying the butter, oil, and popcorn. "Some just lay a dollar or change on the table to donate toward what they eat. People stand around and chat while waiting for the next batch to be popped, buttered and bagged. It goes fast, it's easy, and it's fun," she adds. On other days, Monroe brings in ice cream, cones, cups, and spoons.

> "I am going to keep having fun every day I have left, because there is no other way of life."
>
> —RANDY PAUSCH

Barbara Moy's team at **CaseWare International Inc.**, a software solution company based in Toronto, Canada, gave everyone in the firm a small potted sunflower at their desk. They found it lightened the mood and brightened the office, especially during the winter.

When Jaymie Wahlen was director of success for Chicago, Illinois–based **Dscout**, a customer insight technology provider, she wanted to surprise and reward her team for their work on a beta release. They often joked about going to the Rainforest Cafe, which is down the street from the office. Wahlen sent lunch invitations to her team with the location as "TBD."

> "I think that success is having fun."
>
> —BRUNO MARS

As they were walking past the Rainforest Cafe, she quickly turned right through the front doors. When the team realized the destination, their reaction "was priceless," Wahlen said. "We had a blast sipping on elephant-shaped collector cups and shouting over the periodic 'thunderstorms.' Our conversation landed on childhood birthday parties, so we all took photos together, pretending to be third graders at the best birthday party ever," Wahlen added.

Hayley Benham-Archdeacon worked for **Trader Joe's** when she was a college student. She remembers a time when she was completely overwhelmed and had to call in "studying." As reported in *Business Insider*, she explained the situation to her manager, who replied, "Yeah, that's tough. All right, you want just tomorrow off, or the next day too?" After she apologized for not managing her time better and leaving the team short-staffed, he said, "We'll figure it out. Get an A, OK?" Said Benham-Archdeacon, "Sometimes I still can't believe that really happened."

> "The most effective morale boosters and gestures usually cost little to nothing, as long as they are genuine."
>
> **—THE AUTHORS**

ARE PRANKS FUN?

If you're wondering if "pranks" make for good morale boosters, the answer is, Not very often! Often a prank is an attempt at humor at someone's expense, and that person may well end up taking offense at the prank—and for being the butt of someone else's joke.

Bob can remember working with a client who had a "bonehead award," periodically given to someone who had made a big mistake in their work. Initially, it seemed like fun, but soon someone (deservingly) took offense at receiving the award and was quick to blame others for their actions (and inactions) that contributed to the mistake. They cancelled the award soon after.

Typically, the person who made the mistake is already going to feel bad and perhaps even guilty for the mistake they made. What good is going to come from emphasizing their mistake widely to a larger audience?

Moral of the story: Pranks fail more than they work. They can leave people feeling bad—just the opposite of what should happen—and divide the team when you should be looking for ways to unite everyone in achieving a common mission and goals. More than any other category that is shared in this book, pranks violate our basic Fun principle, that is, "Make it safe and fun for everyone."

THE POWER OF HUMOR: HE OR SHE WHO LAUGHS, LASTS

Fun leads to laughter, an integral by-product of having a good time. And to share the value of laughter, we've tapped the inimitable wordsmith, Richard Lederer, for his insights:

The profound act of laughter is a special blessing to us living in challenging times. The late and beloved humorist Richard Armour contends, "Comedy is as high an art as tragedy. It is as important to make people laugh as to make people cry."

An Apache myth tells us that the Creator made human beings able to walk and talk, to see and hear—to do everything. But the Creator wasn't satisfied. He gifted humans with laughter, and when we laughed and laughed, the Creator said, "Now you are fit to live."

In Navajo culture, there is something called the First Laugh Ceremony. Tradition dictates that each Navajo baby is kept on a cradle board until he or she laughs for the first time. Then the tribe throws a celebration in honor of the child's first laugh, which is considered to be his or her birth as a social being. We are not only *Homo sapiens*, the creature who thinks. We are *Homo guffawus*, the creature who laughs.

"Humor is not a trick," writes former *Prairie Home Companion* host Garrison Keillor. "Humor is a presence in the world—like grace—and shines on everybody." As bread is the staff of life, laughter is its nectar. "A good laugh and a long sleep are the two best cures," winks an Irish adage. "What soap is to the body laughter is to the soul," observes a Yiddish proverb.

Five-year-olds laugh naturally about 250 times a day. How sad it is that as we age, we almost inevitably gain girth and lose mirth. Many of us don't laugh 250 times a month! You don't stop laughing because you grow old. You grow old because you stop laughing.

"Man is the only animal who blushes—or needs to," declared Mark Twain. He could have added, "Man is the only animal that truly laughs—or needs to." Recent studies show that he or she who laughs, lasts. Norman

Cousins, who used laughter to conquer a debilitating disease, wrote, "Illness is not a laughing matter. Perhaps it ought to be. It has always seemed to me that hearty laughter is a good way to jog internally without having to go outdoors."

Scientists affirm what we have known to be true since biblical times: "A merry heart doeth good like a medicine." Laughter can be hazardous to your illness. A belly-shaking guffaw stimulates circulation, tones the muscles, energizes the lungs, excites endorphins, adds T cells in the immune system, relaxes muscle tension, reduces pain and inflammation, boosts the neurotransmitters needed for alertness and memory, stabilizes blood sugar levels, increases motivation to learn, provides superb aerobic exercise—well, you get the idea.

In *Make 'Em Laugh*, Stanford University professor William Fry explains, "When laughter gets to the point where it is convulsive, almost every muscle in the body is involved." According to a Vanderbilt University study, robust laughter burns up 40 calories in 15 minutes and increases metabolism by about 10 percent. You can giggle away about four pounds a year.

Laughter is also an elixir for the mind. It is better to be optimistic than to be a misty optic. Tests administered before and after humor therapy reveal a reduction of stress and depression and a heightened sense of well-being and creativity. More and more, science is discovering that it hurts only when we *don't* laugh. "Laughter is to life what shock absorbers are to automobiles. It won't take the potholes out of the road, but it sure makes the ride smoother," avows Barbara Johnson.

"Laughter is the shortest distance between two people," laughs pianistic comedian Victor Borge. "The most wasted of all days is one without laughter," advises poetry wizard e.e. cummings. Go forth and practice random acts of laughter. One of those acts should be to laugh at yourself. If you can do that, you'll never cease to be amused.

Richard Lederer is a syndicated columnist on language use and author of over 50 books. Used with permission. Contact: richardhlederer@gmail.com; website: verbivore.com.

The CEO of **Acuity**, the financial services company based in Sheboygan, Wisconsin, likes to surprise employees with something small, such as a gift card before the Fourth of July as a thank-you. New hires are invited to social events, including the company holiday party, before they even begin work, getting them incorporated into the friendly, inclusive culture ahead of their first day. The firm also hosts picnics, lunchtime trivia events, and monthly happy hours where family and friends are invited.

As the need arises, workers at San Francisco, California–based **Kimpton Hotel** start impromptu dance parties, take yoga breaks, play in pickup ball games, and set up obstacle courses.

Melissa Grothues, a former manager of company culture at **dTelepathy**, a user-experience design company based in San Diego, California, started a birthday surprise tradition featuring an authentic 4-foot-high Darth Vader piñata. She secretly stuffed it with candy in a storage closet and, one random afternoon, unveiled it to the great surprise and enjoyment of everyone involved. Grothues said, "It was all our team talked about for the rest of the week."

Managers at **Hyland**, a software firm based in Westlake, Ohio, send surprise gifts to remote workers. And one day a year, they drive golf carts to transport employees from parking lots to their offices.

When one of **Uber**'s policy and communications managers passed the California Bar Exam, the day after results were posted, the company's head of

---

5 Ways to Surprise People Positively

1. Email funny messages and photos daily.
2. Give treats and healthy snacks.
3. Give desk candies—chocolate, licorice, gummies, etc.
4. Arrange for on-site 10-minute neck/shoulder massages for team members.
5. Give workers $20 to $100 to decorate their desk in fun ways.

global communications graced Sarah Maxwell's desk with a bottle of champagne, flowers, and a personal note.

When John Ventura was marketing manager for **General Dynamics** Electronics Division, he often took his international customers on tours of San Diego in a rented stretch limousine. One day after dropping his customers off at their hotel, he stopped by the company's fitness center on a whim to pick up a few program participants and staff members in the Champaign Mobile for the premium version of his tour on the town. "I wanted to show other employees what it's like on the other side of corporate life, and we all had a blast," says Ventura.

Colleagues of new hire Chazlee Azevedo of **Evernote**, the note-taking application based in Redwood City, California, decided to throw her a surprise baby shower. "I was so excited when I got the job, and now I'm even more excited," said Azevedo.

When the CEO of **Hyr**, a company that connects short-staffed businesses with more than 20,000 gig workers, heard that an employee had slept poorly before a major meeting because of her bedding, he ordered a set of feather-filled pillows and had them sent to her home. And, when a shift worker took a job at an outdoor market for the holidays, a member of Hyr's floating community team delivered an extra warm jacket for her to wear.

> "The secret to humor is surprise."
> —ARISTOTLE

PART II

Leader-Oriented Fun

Fun at Work is most easily influenced by individual leaders in any organization who are intentional about making fun be a part of work processes and group activities. They know the value of having their workers be excited about their work, and who they are doing it with and for. This better engages their employees and, in the process, creates a work culture that is fun for all.

Employees are drawn to such managers, who get a reputation as being fun to work for and who help make their work easier to do and their jobs ones they better enjoy and look forward to doing every day. When managers demonstrate and encourage fun, it is more likely to be accepted by others.

And if you happen to be working for someone who isn't much fun—don't despair! You can make working on that person part of your agenda to bring him or her along the Fun journey and maybe, just maybe, have that person look good in the process! We are big believers in the power of "managing up."

Any employee can serve as a leader on this topic by stepping up to suggest a fun activity or even leading the charge in making that suggestion come alive and get implemented.

Chapters in this section are "Management Techniques," "Meetings & Office Communication," and "Recognition."

CHAPTER 3

Management Techniques

The key to being a good manager is to keep the people
who hate you away from the ones who are still undecided.

—CASEY STENGEL

The state of management in organizations is generally not good. Officevibe found that three out of four employees report their boss is the worst and most stressful part of their job, and 65 percent of employees say they'd take a new boss over a pay raise.

The average organization is 50 percent as productive as it should be, thanks to less-than-optimal leadership practices. A survey conducted by Interact found that 69 percent of managers are often uncomfortable communicating with employees, and 37 percent said they're uncomfortable having to give direct feedback about their employees' performance if they think the employee might respond negatively to the feedback. When they asked what was most helpful for their career, 72 percent of people said their performance would improve if their managers would provide corrective feedback.

Research from Deloitte University Press found that 86 percent of companies say developing new leaders is an "urgent" need, and 87 percent of companies say they don't do an excellent job developing leaders at all levels. Gallup found 51 percent of managers are disengaged with their job. An additional 14 percent are actively disengaged.

According to other research from Gallup, as a result of poor management, 50 percent of employees leave their companies because of their boss. A Gallup study of 7,272 U.S. adults revealed that one in two had left their job to get away from their manager to improve their overall life at some point in their career.

A bad boss is even bad for your health. In a large-scale study of over 3,000 employees conducted by Anna Nyberg at the Karolinska Institute, results showed a strong link between leadership behavior and heart disease in employees. Stress-producing bosses are literally bad for their employees' hearts.

Having managers loosen up and focus on having more fun at work would surely serve as a positive and practical approach to many of these deficiencies. It would build stronger relationships with their employees and would be a useful skill set to release stress and tension at work, as well as to improve any specific employee interaction, such as providing constructive feedback. Fewer employees would flee poor managers if those managers were more fun loving and actively used fun as a strategy to build the morale of their team and each person who is part of that team.

Let's examine examples of how leaders and managers bring fun into their work groups.

Paul Conningham, a manager with **SBC Global**, uses friendly banter to start discussions with his employees. "I'm a Ford guy and my employee is a Chevy guy," says Conningham. "I might start with something like 'Thank goodness I have a Ford because a Chevy would never have made it through this weather, you must have hitched a ride with someone today, ay?' The exchange only lasted a few minutes, but it sets the tone for the day for us. I'd check to make sure my worker had everything he needed to do his job, and he'd go back to whatever work he was doing. I would go to the next person's workstation and do the same thing. Everyone is different so I would find and most importantly, make a mental note about what motivated each employee and have fun with them about it."

"Healthcare is a serious business but if we don't find time to laugh and enjoy each other's company then it's going to be a very long day. My main personal strategy is to deliberately insert fun comments into conversations," says Naomi Dolahanty, system vice president of talent acquisition for **Advocate Aurora Health** in Milwaukee, Wisconsin. "You can be serious about your work and still have fun! It's not about telling jokes—I'm not good at canned jokes—or giving gifts, but I do that too. It's about engaging and encouraging that levity within the team. As a leader, you set the tone. I truly believe setting a tone of fun and humor allows my team to deliver better results."

Kunji Wang, firm administrator for **Hennelly & Grossfeld LLP** in Los Angeles, California, says, "I try to keep a positive attitude towards work and my coworkers. I see staff get stressed with coworkers or they are unhappy with coworkers where they end up eventually leaving or getting fired. I encourage people not to dwell on the negatives at work and try to remember what they enjoy about their work."

At a party to celebrate a record sales month, Michael Phillips, director of sales for Everett-based **Korry**

> **The Fun at Work Principle: Make It Safe and Fun for Everyone**
>
> Know your people well:
> 1. What they value
> 2. What they consider to be fun
> 3. Then deliver

Electronics, told his sales force that if they set a new record, he'd shave his head. "Everybody got involved in trying to break the record, even the customers," says Phillips. "Returns people were even booking extra rework and warranty sales." When it looked like the record-breaking was sure to happen, Phillips jokingly put up signs on computer monitors saying shaving his head couldn't be done because the computers were down. "That really fueled the fire," he says. He brought in his own "hair terminator" to shave his scalp at the 60th company anniversary party in front of 565 employees, international sales reps, and customers. The highest-performing salespeople got to make the first cuts.

A new employee at Ontario, Canada–based **Learn2-Appreciate** shared, "One time I forgot to move some books he [owner Brian Reynolds] had asked me to. When he saw that it wasn't done he just quietly said, 'My, I wonder why those books are still there?' It actually made me laugh and of course I got it done right away! He was great and never felt demeaning or put down in any way. If I forgot to do something or made a mistake he had a very lighthearted way of dealing with it—in a way that didn't make me feel bad."

"When I was in the military and faced with a big challenge—I found myself literally and figuratively digging through many tools in my management toolkit," said Dee Williams. "One thing that helped me stay humble and grounded particularly was this beanie bag doughboy that my husband gave me." The doughboy proved to be an invaluable mascot

> "In most cases being a good boss means hiring talented people and then getting out of their way."
>
> —TINA FEY

and sidekick during that time and even after Williams retired. Why the doughboy? "One of my favorite commercials is the doughboy in the airport who goes through security, gets patted down but keeps giggling. He says, 'I'll get it together' and goes back through to get checked again. And hard as he tries to stifle his giggles they come out (more of a chortle). He's somewhat embarrassed but you know I laughed so hard that I cried the first time I saw it. Then I stopped crying and thought about how many times I felt like the doughboy trying to 'get it together.'

"I began to use that as an analogy when I counseled and mentored my junior leaders during times when either they or a subordinate made a mistake. I've had some of my junior leaders who now are senior military leaders and/or successful civilian leaders, business owners, etc. And I think about how many doughboy experiences that we all had together and we got it together. And look at us now. That little doughboy was a mascot that I had with me in many offices, positions—even took him with me when I deployed as a civilian to Kuwait and Iraq—and he reminded me in his own cute little doughboy way that 'I'll get it together.'"

At **Takezō**, makers of customized nutrition supplements, cofounder Reid Block says: "We frequently do 'walk and talks' in the woods, as well as hit the gym for work. Sometimes it is tough to take notes, but we manage. We believe that it helps us get into that flow state. When a cofounder and I lived in close proximity we would often hit the tennis court and have a

> ### 5 Fun Individual Management Techniques
>
> 1. Be a good listener.
> 2. Be the first to do something fun. Be a good sport.
> 3. Encourage others to have fun.
> 4. Encourage regular team events.
> 5. Hone your humor skills and start each team meeting with a joke.

> "I view my role more as trying to set up an environment where personalities, creativity, and individuality of all the different employees come out and can shine."
>
> —TONY HSIEH

lot of great business conversations where new ideas were born and projects funded."

When he managed the housekeeping department before becoming CEO, Mike DeFrino of **Kimpton Hotels** gave daily pep talks to his 40+ staff members. He would then join them in stripping rooms and scrubbing toilets. "To build trust and credibility with employees, it's important to walk the walk and get some mud on your boots," says DeFrino.

Attorney Susan Frankel tells of a fun program instituted at **AAA** of Southern California called Dump a Dog, where workers who finished a project could pass an assignment they least wanted to handle on to their manager. The program stemmed from a holiday contest, but its potential as a widespread reward for completing a successful case or outstanding work was quickly realized. The program was both a motivator for higher performance and a fun way for management to show they really were there to help.

Zack Ottenstein, president, sales and marketing, for **The Image Group** in Toledo, Ohio, reports: "My partner and I used to walk around the office and congratulate each other for a 'Big Day.' I wanted to get all of our team members in on the fun. So I started walking through our office every morning greeting each team member and saying 'Good morning. It's a big day!' It became our rally cry. Whenever I walk past people in the hallway, they look at me and say with a smile, 'Big Day!' We printed T-shirts that say 'It's A BIG, BIG, BIG Day' with our company logo and

6 More Fun Individual Management Techniques

1. Have your team create a fun skit for the next all-hands meeting.

2. Switch places with an employee for a day or so.

3. Wash an associate's vehicle in the company parking lot when they reach a goal.

4. Ask your employees what could be done to make their work more fun.

5. Take a breath and remember to lighten up.

6. Hire fun-friendly people.

shipped them to every employee's home during the pandemic's stay-at-home order. Team members now tell each other congratulations on a BIG Day. They also come to share with me when they're having a BIG Day. Adding a little fun in the morning about a Big Day made a BIG difference at The Image Group!"

"Do unto others the way they want to be done unto."
—MILTON BENNETT

For several hours on Sundays, former CEO Frank Blake of Atlanta, Georgia–based **Home Depot**, a home improvement retailer, would handwrite thank-you notes to high-achieving employees—from hourly associates up to division managers. In every note he specifically mentioned why the achievement mattered to the customer, team, and/or organization.

CASE STUDY

DISNEY MANAGERS REACH OUT

When surveyed, The Walt Disney World Swan & Dolphin Resort employees reported that managers weren't around much when things were busiest.

To solve this challenge, the company initiated "five-minute chats" where all managers were assigned 10 employees each who didn't report to them. Each manager took time in the next two weeks to visit and chat with each of their 10 assignees to find out how things were going, to see if they had any questions, etc. Managers got to interact with workers they typically didn't know, employees loved it, and everyone felt closer to one another.

One executive took the practice even further. During the winter holiday season, Bob Small, VP of Disney Resorts in Orlando, Florida, used to work "small shifts" on Christmas Eve. He would join the laundry workers in washing and folding clothes. He'd say, "If they've got to be here and not with their families, the least I could do is be here too."

Virgin Group founder and CEO Richard Branson has always tried to say hello to every employee when he visited the different locations. Some offices had over one thousand employees. If he missed them at work, he would often call them on Saturday morning to thank them for their work.

Former **Twitter** CEO Dick Costolo led a Managing at Twitter session at least once a quarter. Instead of using slides, Costolo shared stories and his own best practices and kept managers engaged through role-playing activities. He also shared his leadership philosophy, influencing them to use and share his techniques with others.

At **Quantum Workplace**, an Omaha, Nebraska–based employee engagement software company, CEO Greg Harris is known to have spontaneous Indian leg-wrestling contests with other workers, including other executives. He also initiates company dodgeball and wears colonial wigs to distribute the company's "Constitution" handbook.

Each office of the **Kimley-Horn Design** firm based in Raleigh, North Carolina, has an official VP of Fun, who organizes ice cream parties and paper-airplane contests.

Alexia Bregman, cofounder and CEO of Solana Beach, California–based natural energy drink company **Vuka**, looks for unique ways to connect with employees. One thing she and cofounder-husband Darian Bregman did was to implement WOMP—What's On My Plate. Bregman meets weekly with each worker to create a to-do list. "We don't really mind where or when these are completed, but when we meet the following week, we look at that list again and see how each individual employee is doing," Bregman says. "It's a great way of giving employees autonomy while still staying on top of what they're doing without micromanaging."

Evernote, a note-taking application firm based in Redwood City, California, has an "officer training program" where employees "crash" two meetings each week and ask whatever questions they want—even in departments they don't work in.

> "Rank does not confer privilege or give power. It imposes responsibility."
>
> **—PETER F. DRUCKER**

On his Humor at Work blog, Aaron McDaniel wrote about how to stop all the complaining that workers did on the job: When he managed unionized call center reps, they worked hard but also complained excessively, which had a negative influence on team morale. He came up with a great strategy: At each team meeting, he added a standing agenda item called the "venting session" when reps could complain about anything. All he did was listen, take notes, and ask clarifying questions to understand their points of view. The first session took over an hour. Between meetings he would solve some of the issues they brought up, and report back to them in the next meeting. They discussed the things that would change, and the items that wouldn't. Over time, the venting session took less and less time, to the point that no one had anything to complain about. Reps became more satisfied, and their quality of work improved.

> "You do not lead by hitting people over the head—that's assault, not leadership."
>
> **—DWIGHT EISENHOWER**

One day, CEO Kay Fittes of **High-Heeled Success** in Cincinnati, Ohio, got a call from a client. "We have a huge problem!" said the client, who operated an Early Childhood Learning Center run on a traditional school system calendar. The program was changing to be year-round, and this made many teachers unhappy. "They weren't getting rich as teachers, but one perk had been their summers off! They were seething about losing their summers," said Fittes. "My mandate was to enable them to see things differently. We whined together, mourned together and finally brainstormed together. What could make this a fun place for summer?

"Visions of sand, water, umbrellas came to mind. Yep, that would help. Picture it, the first day of the summer session: all staff arriving with sunglasses on, a beach chair to place in their classroom, Beach Boys' music playing in the background and lots of water activities with the kids. For the gutsy ones, shorts were permitted. Plus, on the walls were summer posters, beach scenes and summer-happy wall quotes." Every teacher was encouraged to have extra "summery" fun-themed activities.

Where did Fittes's inspiration come from? When she considered attitude, loss, fear, and fun, she remembered her daughter's first day of kindergarten. "As many children are, she was anxious about what 'real school' would be like. The first words out of her mouth when she came home that first day on the big yellow bus were, 'I'm going to like school!' Why? Her principal, Mrs. Deters, had cruised through the halls of Dumont Elementary School on roller skates. Can you imagine what it was like to be a teacher and a student in that school? Obviously, it made an impression on me, as it was the first thought that came to mind when I was tasked with shifting the workplace attitude. We know that a fun atmosphere encourages creativity, free thinking and stress relief. What could be your version of a summer fun atmosphere or a roller-skating principal in your workplace?"

From their surveys and task analyses, **Matsushita Kotobuki Electronics** in Vancouver, Washington, found that varying the work assignments in their assembly plant keeps jobs more fun and interesting and helps reduce injuries. The company assembles hard disc and DVD multi-drives, and while robotic devices perform some of the work, most of the assembly steps require the human touch. Job rotations helped increase the variety of tasks as workers took on more duties. Employees at Matsushita rotate to four different workstations each shift, spending two hours at each shift, and then rotate to different workstations throughout the week. Every three weeks, workers also change assembly lines.

To better engage her staff in a fun way, Courtney Bowens, director of operations for **The Retina Group** of Washington, includes them in the development of new ideas. For example, when she wanted to create a remote position for surgical scheduling, she formed a focus group of current schedulers to discuss the pros and cons of creating the position. "Everyone had good ideas and even provided me with thoughts that

"The human race has only one effective weapon—and that is laughter."
—**MARK TWAIN**

I wasn't contemplating because my approach is 30k feet instead of being involved with specifics of many of the daily tasks. The front line are the best historians to share their experiences. This in turn has helped me to create the best possible scenario for starting this new position."

CHAPTER 4

Meetings & Office Communication

It's amazing what you're saying to others when you just listen.

—THOMAS FRIEDMAN

It's no surprise that most office workers spend a large amount of their time at work in meetings. According to *Inc.* and the online meeting company Fuze, there are 25 million meetings per day in the U.S., making up 15 percent of an organization's collective time, with the average employee spending up to four hours per week simply preparing for status update meetings.

They also found that most meetings are unproductive; in fact, executives consider more than 67 percent of meetings a failure, costing businesses more than $37 billion per year for unproductive meetings. Other estimates are even higher. According to Doodle's State of Meetings Report, the cost of poorly organized meetings was $399 billion in the U.S. in a recent year, representing a tremendous drag on the effectiveness of businesses.

And other forms of communication at work fare no better. For example, The Radicati Group found that, every day, 205.6 billion emails are sent across the globe, only one-third of which are actually opened. Around 25 percent of employees think email is a major productivity killer, although 74 percent of all adults online prefer email as their main method of communication, as mentioned by Ving.

David Grossman reported in "The Cost of Poor Communications" that a survey of 400 companies with 100,000 employees each cited an average loss per company of $62.4 million per year because of inadequate communication to and between employees. And in her article "The Top Ten Email Blunders That Cost Companies Money," Debra Hamilton asserted that miscommunication cost smaller companies of 100 employees an average of $420,000 per year.

Would meetings and other forms of communication become more effective and efficient if they were a little more fun? We believe so.

Let's look at some examples of how companies make meetings and communications a bit more fun for everyone involved, helping participants get excited about communicating with each other rather than dreading the task.

At **The Ken Blanchard Companies**, the authors came up with the idea of rotating responsibility for bringing in a joke to their weekly meeting. It started the meeting out on a fun note, people had a week to come up with a joke, and everyone shared responsibility for the humor, making it even more fun. They also experimented with other tactics, including timers to stay on agenda and standing meetings, which always tended to be short!

At the start of weekly staff meetings, Maria Gonzales, the manager of the **Memorial Branch Library** in San Antonio, Texas, has her team play a game where Gonzalez writes down a number and folds it up. Then everyone calls out a number, and whoever guesses the correct or nearest to the correct number becomes "It" and is encouraged to tell the group a joke, sing a song, or do some other fun or silly thing to help the team relax.

Open Systems Technologies, a Grand Rapids, Michigan–based company, holds paper-airplane contests during their meetings.

Plum Organics, a baby food manufacturer headquartered in Emeryville, California, distributes coloring books and crayons for team members to use at Thursday meetings.

New York City–based **Fast Company**, the business magazine, has Monopoly game–themed meeting rooms.

"Before COVID hit we needed to give a presentation to a group of people," says Linda Mott from **BC Hydro**. Rather than create a PowerPoint, they developed their own version of an "escape room" where attendees solved puzzles and opened locks in order to get to a prize at the end. "It was a fun way to learn and was fun putting it together," says Mott.

What if you go to a business meeting and a Wii bowling game breaks out? That's what happened to Tiffany Griffiths, an employee of **Business Solutions Inc.**, an information system consulting firm headquartered in The Woodlands, Texas. "It's a lot of fun," says Griffiths. "It's a way to get creative, to do things differently," says Tiffany's manager, Daron Brown. When not bowling, many "walking" meetings are held outside to take advantage of the fresh air.

CASE STUDY

WHO DONE IT? GROUP ICEBREAKER

Fareast Mercantile Trade Company Ltd. in Lagos, Nigeria, had great fun with a "who done it?" icebreaker during a company leadership meeting. The facilitator (Bob) distributed a checklist of various personal descriptions, traits, and activities to attendees and asked them to interview as many other attendees as possible over a 15-minute timeframe. The checklist included items such as:

- Lives with parents or grandparents

- Has a pet animal

- Has children under the age of nineteen

- Plays a musical instrument

- Has been married over twenty years

- Loves to cook

- Taught at a college or university

- Has visited 5 or more African countries

The goal of the interview was to find out which descriptions fit the person being interviewed, and to check off as many as possible. During the debrief of the activity, people with similar interests were grouped together to discuss specific questions and further share about common experiences.

The group enjoyed the activity so much that members continued the activity during lunch and into the evening. They found it was a great way to connect with and learn more about their colleagues. It's a small, small world.

Virgin founder Richard Branson believes that innovative ideas come from innovative spaces. For example, holding a meeting in a park or cafe will inject freshness and create new ideas and ways of thinking.

Workers at **Genera Games**, a mobile game publisher headquartered in Seville, Spain, have meetings while warming up and playing a quick game of basketball. And management team meetings at **Nugget Markets**, a Woodland, California–based grocery chain, have been known to be held in wrestling rings.

Simple Truth, a brand development agency based in Chicago, Illinois, puts a different spin on conventional meetings as well. They hold a 9@9 Meeting every Monday—a nine-minute-long meeting starting at 9 a.m. At **TINYpulse**, an employee engagement software provider based in Seattle, Washington, the daily staff meeting starts at 8:48 a.m. Both companies have found that employees seldom miss or are late for these meetings.

Evergage, the cloud-based software firm located in Somerville, Massachusetts, has 15-minute daily meetings but has found they usually only last between 5 and 15 minutes. And they end with a bang by having team members do push-ups. The unusual approach caught on, and they all really like it, and push-ups have become a tradition.

Workers at **Asana**, a team collaboration application company, and **Airbnb**, the vacation housing provider in San Francisco, California, never have meetings on Wednesdays. **Hugo**, the meeting notes developer based in San Francisco, California, cut its meetings down to four hours per week. By using its own product along with video and Slack, the company found its employees were better informed than when they relied more on traditional meetings.

Workers are rarely late to meetings at the Inquisium division of **Cvent**, a survey software firm headquartered in the greater Washington, D.C., area. VP Darrell Gehrt started the unique custom of having latecomers sing when they arrive. "We've heard the national anthem, happy birthday, and nursery rhymes. The biggest downside is that it has been so effective, we rarely get the opportunity to make anyone sing these days," says Gehrt.

> "Only hold meetings where two pizzas are enough to feed everyone in the room."
> **—AMAZON**

Brivo, a Bethesda, Maryland–based security management software firm, has a "no rehash" rule. Meeting attendees raise the "No Rehash" Ping-Pong paddle to let others know that a topic or point has already been addressed or made. "It's a visual reminder, but more importantly it empowers everyone in the company to call out counterproductive rehashing whenever and wherever they see it," says president and CEO Steve Van Till, who started the rule. "The bigtime savings is that no one has to justify invoking the rule itself, and the meeting can proceed with earlier decisions intact."

Along a similar vein, at **The Ken Blanchard Companies**, an Escondido, California–based management and leadership training firm, the authors used a coconut as a prop to facilitate discussions. Whoever held the coconut could speak without interruption. It helped keep the balance of speaking and listening in meetings. And it turned into an enduring communication tool and an endearing part of every meeting. At **Microsoft**, one team uses "Ralph," a rubber chicken, to toss among the group to the speaker of the moment.

Creative director C. J. Johnson of Santa Monica, California–based **Buddytruk**, a mobile app that connects truck owners with one another, says, "If we run over, the last person talking has to do 50 push-ups. At first it was just a funny gag. Now, it's turned into a great bonding experience."

Stopwatches are set for 30 minutes at the start of every meeting at San Francisco, California–based **Tripping.com**, a search engine for vacation rentals. If the meeting goes longer, the person who called the meeting must throw $5 in the team "swear" jar. Business development consulting firm **Just Fearless**, headquartered in Los Angeles, California, also sets a 30-minute time limit for meetings. Founder Kisha Mays says if the meeting runs long, the chairs are removed, and everyone must stand until the end. This idea is not lost on the top tech companies. **Facebook**'s engineering manager, Mark Tonkelowitz, reportedly holds 15-minute stand-up meetings at 12 p.m. daily. The impending lunchtime makes for concise updates.

Perhaps fearing "death by PowerPoint," CEO and founder of online retailer **Amazon**, Jeff Bezos, has

8 Ways to Make Meetings More Fun

1. Don't call it a meeting. Call it a "schlubfest."

2. Hold meetings outside or in a park.

3. Start a meeting with the singing of a well-known song, giving a prize to anyone who can sing it without missing a word.

4. Assign a different team member to tell a joke at team meetings.

5. Bring toys to spur creative thinking.

6. As an icebreaker, ask each member to share two truths and one lie about him/herself. The others must guess which is the lie. Give out prizes.

7. To keep attendees engaged, add something humorous every few minutes.

8. Have fun-loving facilitators run major meetings/retreats.

banned the visual aid application in his meetings. He believes the tool makes things easy for presenters but more difficult for the audience.

Strategic planning consultant Michele Tamayo, of **Tamayo Group Inc.**, a Cardiff-by-the-Sea, California, consulting firm, shared two fun icebreaker examples she used during COVID-19:

> "You want to go to work with people you like and where everyone is having fun."
>
> —MEGAN FOX

When the **State Association of County Retirement Systems** (California) held a recent virtual board meeting, the facilitator asked attendees to share one "day in the life" example from their jobs along with one hobby or interest they had outside of work. After one member said that he played the bagpipes, another member urged him to play for them at the next meeting break. People were amazed and very interested in how long he had been playing, where he'd played, and so on.

To open a virtual board meeting of the **San Diego County Bar Association**, members shared a positive experience during the viral outbreak. One member proudly presented a diamond engagement ring, while another asked her husband to introduce their newborn baby. "At both meetings, everyone was very engaged, and it really opened up the conversation with several follow-up questions. They really got to know one another much better," says Tamayo.

Meeting attendees at **Poll Everywhere**, the San Francisco, California–based company that collects live responses through their online services, have a "moment of Zen," where they take time, as a group, to learn something new or reflect on the meeting or their day. Leaders and facilitators share inspiring quotes or stories, and team members discuss wins and highlights and compliment others.

When she worked for **Time Warner** in Milwaukee, Noelle Sment used an effective stress management strategy: a Bad Day Board. She would list everyone's name with a magnet that could be moved to show who was under a lot of stress, experiencing personal problems, struggling with difficult customers, etc. Initially meant to serve as a warning system for others, the group soon started cheering up anyone who was having a "bad day" and had a lot of fun in the process!

Barbara Ashkin of Syracuse, New York–based **Cxtec**, a technology infrastructure provider, added humor to the company's phone-answering menu that—in addition to the expected options—said, "Press 4 to hear the lion roar. Press 5 to hear a funny joke." "Customers appreciated the humor and realized that this is a different kind of company," says Ashkin.

At the Seattle, Washington, offices of **Hulu**, the company encourages transparently sharing information in a variety of ways: via Huluverse (the company's social intranet), video conferencing, chat rooms, monthly company-wide meetings called "wind downs," or good old-fashioned face time with coworkers.

At Emeryville, California–headquartered **Pixar**, the animation and entertainment studio, workers participate in Note's Day. The company puts current projects on pause to have company-wide brainstorming

7 Ways to Have Better Meetings

1. Send agendas well in advance of the meeting.
2. Use an icebreaker.
3. Recognize people's achievements (start of the meeting).
4. Have a clear objective, ground rules.
5. Take notes.
6. Invite only necessary attendees.
7. Keep them short.

sessions. People gather in small teams to share ideas and discuss relevant issues and company challenges. Leaders from various departments drop into other teams' meetings to understand and hear the varying viewpoints.

"We believe in work+life, not work vs. life."

—DHARMESH SHAH

Facebook holds "hackathons"—employees collaborate intensely on tech-related projects over a finite period of time—throughout the year, and they have not only become a great way for employees to interact and work together, but have resulted in the creation of several beneficial features such as tagging friends in Facebook comments and "liking" friends' posts.

To inspire direct interactions with his workforce, Charles Phillips, CEO of **Infor**, a software company headquartered in New York City, gives his cell phone number to all employees, encouraging them to call or text whenever they wish.

At **Moz**, the Seattle, Washington–based marketing analytics software firm, CEO Rand Fishkin strives for complete transparency, including the type of information he shares on his blog—from multi-million-dollar business deal failures to his proposal to his future wife. Employees have found it very inspirational and have become more transparent themselves.

Sridhar Vembu, founder of **Zoho**, a software development company headquartered in Chennai, India, relies on a tool called Cideo to transparently communicate with his company. He uses an A.M.A. (ask me anything) format to respond to both spontaneous and prepared questions.

At New York City–based **Bitly**, a URL shortening service, CEO Mark Josephson connects with his employees on a daily basis by sitting at different tables and desks throughout the office. But it's his Cocktails & Dreams meetings where he finds some of the best engagement. Every week, someone is nominated to be a bartender, and everyone in the company grabs a drink together, while Josephson gives an update. "We meet weekly to share updates and progress as a company," says Josephson. "We celebrate wins and acknowledge losses. It's ultimately a great way to recap the week and set the stage for the following week," he adds.

Mark Dankberg, CEO of the Carlsbad, California–based broadband services and technology company **ViaSat**, started Mark D's Book Club, where workers can read books on business, strategy, leadership, and innovation. The idea was started as a way for the company's global team to learn the same business concepts and language, think strategically together, and exchange ideas. "It has become a way for ViaSat employees to better understand how we think, how we view the world, and how we make decisions," says Dankberg. "And it helps each employee be more prepared in shaping their own career development."

CEO Harry Herington, of information service provider **NIC Inc.**, a digital government service provider

7 More Ways to Have Better Meetings

1. Give a variety of food. Meet and Eat!
2. Incorporate a team-building activity.
3. Change the scenery; meet in different venues.
4. Switch seating order.
5. Rotate roles (facilitator, timekeeper, scribe, eraser monitor).
6. Use breakout groups.
7. Meet standing up.

"If you had to identify in one word the reason why the human race has not achieved and never will achieve its full potential, that word would be 'meetings.'"

—DAVE BARRY

from Olathe, Kansas, has fun and promotes employee engagement by visiting NIC branches across the company via motorcycle. He calls his initiative Ask the CEO, and the idea was born to ensure open communication in the aftermath of the 2001 Enron scandal. "How do you get someone to trust you? You look them in the eye," says Herington, who hosts a dinner during his visit. Workers are encouraged to ask him any business and nonbusiness questions.

CHAPTER 5

Recognition

People often say that motivation doesn't last. Well neither does bathing. That's why we recommend it daily.

—ZIG ZIGLAR

Few things feel as good as being thanked or praised by someone else at work for having done a good job, yet it happens far less often than it should in most work environments. Gallup found 65 percent of employees haven't received any form of recognition for good work in the last year. Reward Gateway found 85 percent of employees think managers and leaders should spot good work and give praise in the moment, and 81 percent of employees think this should happen on a continuous, year-round basis. This survey also found that 70 percent of employees say that motivation and morale would improve "massively" if managers simply started saying thank you more.

A survey by OGO found that the lack of recognition has a massively negative impact on how employees feel about the workplace. According to the survey, 82 percent of American professionals feel that they aren't adequately recognized for their contribution.

In another study, when asked what leaders could do more of to improve engagement, a Psychometrics survey found 58 percent of respondents replied "give recognition," and a survey by Socialcast found 69 percent of employees said they would work harder if they felt their efforts were better appreciated.

Employees also typically value praise more than other tangible forms of reward, including cash. According to a study by Officevibe, 82 percent of employees think it's better to give someone praise than a gift.

Employees want to appreciate each other as well. When offered a simple tool to do so, 44 percent of all workers will provide peer recognition on an ongoing basis, according to an Employee Engagement Report by Globoforce. Peer-to-peer recognition is powerful—it's nearly 36 percent more likely to have a positive impact on financial results than manager-only recognition, according to the Society for Human Resources Management.

The ways employees can be thanked, recognized, and praised are extensive. Let's look at some creative examples of what others have done—and you can, as well!

A worker at **LaSalle**, the Chicago, Illinois–headquartered global real estate investment firm, suggested a new way for her teammates to "pay it forward." After a Zoom meeting, they each sent an encouraging note to the person whose face was on the screen below them.

Sandy Hackenwerth, an employee of **Maritz Inc.** located in Fenton, Missouri, says that when she gets to a meeting early and is waiting for others to arrive, she uses that time to jot thank-you notes to other employees for their help. And when individuals in the company are promoted, she always sends them each a note congratulating them on their success.

When large projects are launched, Jill Boone, the assistant vice president of European talent development for Surrey, United Kingdom–based **Enterprise Holdings**, sends thank-you notes to stakeholders, including all who worked on the project, to recognize their specific contributions. In a separate note, she asks stakeholders to send a thank-you specifically to those who worked on the project. "I always give credit to the person who had the idea, who took the lead, who was willing to share with our team, and not keep the idea to themselves," says Boone.

> "What gets recognized, gets repeated."
> —THE AUTHORS

Alissa Meredith, lead physical therapist for **Scripps Memorial Hospital** in Encinitas, California, instituted a Margarita Award for the therapist who had to work with the toughest client that week or month. The awardee was then treated by the group to a margarita happy hour.

Workers at **CultureIQ**, the New York City–headquartered culture management company, ended each week with a round of handshakes—or fist bumps—to thank everyone for their work. "[It] started right after we launched," says company CEO Greg Besner, according to *Inc.* "It was a Friday, the team was working so hard, and it just felt like an act of respect needed to happen. Now it's a tradition."

> "When you start recognizing that you're having fun, life can be delightful."
> —JANE BIRKIN

Ron Sutton, CEO of **Standard Auto Parts Corp**. in Baltimore, Maryland, asked his managers to submit recent positive achievements that their groups accomplished that they were proud of. After they submitted an item, he gave them tickets to attend a special meeting where they applauded each example shared. Sutton challenged the group to make the response to each item louder than the previous one.

Soon, the entire group was standing and cheering—sending a positive surge that spread throughout the company.

As a leadership development consultant, Don Stuckey ensures that managers understand the importance of showing appreciation to employees. He tells them to find someone on their team to appreciate each day. "I encourage managers to do it in staff meetings, small groups, or stand-up meetings so others realize the importance of appreciation," says Stuckey. When he coaches leaders of an organization, he includes appreciation as part of the process. "I model appreciation for them, teach them how and how often to do it, and stress the importance of them as executives of the organization to be solid appreciation role models. Middle managers learn by observing executive managers' important behaviors to deliver."

At the start of every meeting, even one-to-ones, the **Crabtree Group**, a dental practice management firm located in Winchester, Tennessee, recognizes achievements. "Focusing on the successes before jumping into what's going on helps with maintaining positive energy in the company," says President Patty Crabtree.

At **Red Velvet Events**, the creative planning agency located in Austin, Texas, every Monday is the big day for recognizing high-performing individuals. During the weekly staffing meeting, one team member was given Pockets, a 90s-era troll doll, to adorn their work area. The previous week's recipient would nominate the next, publicly acknowledging that employee for

---

5 Most Memorable Ways to Recognize Workers

In a recent Gallup workplace survey, employees were asked what types of recognition were the most memorable for them. Most employees prefer employee recognition in the form of:

1. Public recognition via award or certificate

2. Private recognition from a boss, peer, or customer

3. Recognized achievements through evaluations or reviews

4. Promotion or increase in scope of work or responsibility to show trust

5. Monetary award such as a trip, prize, or pay increase

why they deserved the award. Winners would further customize the doll with jewelry, add tattoos, and even create a castle for it to live in. Several years later, they'd gone through five totems and decided to change from the doll to a hand-painted denim jacket. Now winners drape the jacket over the backs of their chairs for a week.

SnackNation CEO Sean Kelly says that "it's important to call people out for doing something awesome because there's awesome occurrences around us every single day." At 4:30 p.m. every Friday at this Culver City, California–based snacking-experience company, all hands get together for Crush It Friday. They have music, drinks, and dancing. They gather in a circle and people volunteer to crush somebody. "They recognize somebody else for an awesome accomplishment that they saw that person do that embodied a core value of the organization," adds Kelly. Then they offer what they are grateful for. "After 30, 40 minutes, the feeling is just fantastic and it sends people into the weekends on a high note where they then go and share that story with their friends and family and they bring gratitude and recognition into their home life. It's this virtuous cycle that just keeps getting better."

At **Zoom Video Communications**, headquartered in San Jose, California, the Happiness Crew ensures that each office is set up to recognize their high-performing employees quarterly. During these all-hands meetings, photos of and short stories about individuals are shared with everyone. "It's huge for morale," says Anna Pinckney, an order desk lead in sales. "Sometimes we move so quickly to help each other out that we forget how big of an impact we make on the individual and the department."

Birdhouse, the intranet of **Twitter**, the social media company based in San Francisco, California, enables workers to send recognition tweets to other employees. Tweets include recipients' photos and a short blurb on why they are being recognized.

> "If you want employees to feel appreciated, you need to celebrate their achievements regularly and publicly."
>
> —**LOGAN GREEN**

The Walt Disney Company in Burbank, California, created the #castcompliment social media recognition program that allows guests to recognize cast members via Twitter. These tweets not only go on Twitter for the world to see, but are also placed in employees' formal records so leaders can see them.

> "I can live for two months on a good compliment."
>
> —**MARK TWAIN**

At Mountain View, California–based technology giant **Google**, workers use a company-built app called gThanks. The app encourages employees to publicly thank each other for exemplary work. They also created a low-tech, no-cost version called the Wall of Happy. It hangs outside the office of the Wall's creator, Lazlo Bock.

Crowe, a professional services firm located in Chicago, Illinois, provides a way for clients—through an online survey—to give the names of Crowe employees who have served them well. Once they are identified, the survey generates a Recognize Alert. The firm extends the alerts with a Pay It Forward program, where recognized people can praise others who helped to serve the clients but weren't named on the survey. All names of Recognize Alert and Pay It Forward recipients are then shared on the Crowe Newswire On Demand to reinforce in others what a good job looks like.

When a caller is impeccably served by an employee of **Capital One**'s Tampa Bay call center and wants to tell that person's manager about it, the company awards the employee with a shiny Mylar balloon, which is then tied to the employee's desk chair.

"One of our clients, National Business Capital in New York City, has a wonderful culture for recognition, and puts a big paper thermometer up in the office showing daily and weekly sales," says Sunny Grosso, culture chief for **DeliveringHappiness.com**. They bang a gong for each sale. When the temperature gets to the boiling point, they celebrate everything that made it possible.

"I had poker chips made up with our logo on one side and I WENT ABOVE & BEYOND on the other side," says Sean Mahoney, president of **Suburban Custom Awards & Framing** in Decatur, Georgia. "I hand these out to an employee(s) that put in added effort, received praise from a customer, stayed late when needed, or ensured a deadline was met." The chip entitles workers to one hour of paid time off. Most of them accumulate the chips and take a half day off or use them to run personal errands. "While it's not a new idea, it just shows that recognition is important and will reap benefits to all involved."

5 Ways to Have Fun Recognition

1. Give someone deserving a standing ovation.

2. Insert candid photos of workers at company events into PowerPoint.

3. Create a yearbook for your team with pictures and stories of good work.

4. When a worker meets a formal goal, let them spin a wheel for a reward.

5. Ring a gong when a big sale/major achievement is made.

CASE STUDY

THE ULTIMATE IN PEER-DRIVEN, HEARTFELT AWARDS

Do your formal award programs lack freshness, excitement, or personal meaning? Most do. In fact, research shows that program freshness is one of the primary concerns reported by most organizations that have formal recognition programs. If stale programs are a challenge for your organization as well, consider trying the ultimate peer- and company value–driven, heartfelt awards process like the one used by then San Diego–based General Dynamics (GD) and by Escondido, California–headquartered The Ken Blanchard Companies. Both programs were started by Mario, and the one at KBC was eventually directed and improved by Todd Willer, who took the process to greater heights—year on year, average participation was 66 percent of the total company.

Why Do It?

Both programs had two key objectives: (1) create formal awards based on the core values of our company/programs, and (2) do it in a way that yields exceptional personal meaning.

How Does It Work?

The secret to the process is that it is employee driven. Employees nominate people for awards, validate nominations, select winners, make the awards, and present them. After publicizing the awards and what to look for, workers are encouraged to "catch people doing things right." There are several awards per company value. Employees nominate peers for the awards for specific work behaviors that result in effective outcomes—that is, actions that get the organization and themselves closer to their goals. And they do it in a way that promotes their core values. Awards are given out as part of a banquet, lunch, or dinner in an Academy Award–style program. The overall result is that people are encouraged to continue working with each other, for the company, and for themselves.

Award Example

General Dynamics' Timex Person of the Year Award to promote a "perseverance" value is still one of the most popular and meaningful awards. It is a hybrid of *Time* magazine's "Person of the Year" and Timex's classic ad campaign about the watch that "takes a licking but keeps on ticking."

Validation & Selection Process

A volunteer group of employees use a nomination sheet and check out to see if things happened as claimed, and once the claims are verified, they make a slate of the top nominations for each award. Then everyone votes (online). Numbers are tabulated and winners are identified—but not announced until the awards event. And here's where the exceptional "personal meaning" happens—where people feel genuine honor and appreciation.

Employee-Made Awards & Presentations

Instead of giving typical plaques and certificates, a group of employee volunteers—many of whom nominated eventual winners—use their creative skills to recycle items from attics, garages, storage units, and thrift shops. They customize each award specifically to the winner's personality and the story behind getting the award, which makes the award more meaningful for winners. Recycled items are strongly encouraged for two reasons: (1) recycled items are a metaphor for employees and the company to renew their energy and commitment to doing meaningful work, and (2) they cut cost significantly. Each award is usually made for under $20.

And what they make is fascinating: from paintings, sculptures, T-shirts, and baby shoes to songs, books, and scrolls.

Nominators of award winners have the right of first refusal to make awards for their winners. They also have the same right to present their creations to the winners. This is where the meaning goes deep. For example, at the inaugural awards event held at The Ken Blanchard Companies, the first award presenter

continues on next page

(for Timex Person of the Year) was someone who had made the award she was to present. She got pretty emotional in sharing what the award winner had done and how that influenced how she created the award. When the award winner got to the stage, both presenter and winner cried and hugged each other, while the whole company—about 250 people at the time—gave them a standing ovation. This occurs at every event. For every award, there are at least two individual winners, besides the company. Volunteers love making the award, and winners appreciate the extra thought and effort put in by their peers. It's something a gift catalog cannot do.

It may seem that asking employees to create awards would cause a lot of pressure on them—to make sure the awards were of professional quality. But that concern has never been an issue over the 35 years this process has been used. People have fun with the awards: what they are given for and how they are made. For example, the "Timex" award ended up being an oversized, smashed Timex watch, glued back together and mounted on a varnished board with a little brass plate for the award name, the person's name, and the date. All work done by the volunteer. Of all the awards, plaques, and certificates a person receives over the years, the ones made from the heart tend to be the ones that touch another's heart.

At shipping giant **UPS** from Atlanta, Georgia, drivers who go 25 years without an accident are inducted into the company's Circle of Honor and given a special patch and a bomber jacket.

HubSpot, the developer and marketing firm from Cambridge, Massachusetts, awards its high-achieving employees with the JEDI Award, an engraved sword.

> "To pursue anything, you've got to have fun with it and never give up on it."
>
> —KAETLYN OSMOND

Chevron U.S.A., headquartered in San Ramon, California, keeps a large box secured with a padlock, brimming with all sorts of gifts. An employee who is recognized on the spot for an accomplishment is brought to the Treasure Chest by his or her supervisor, who holds the keys. The employee can choose an item from the box—a coffee mug, pen-and-pencil set, gift certificate, coupon for lunch or dinner, or movie tickets. Recognition can come from peers as well.

Warby Parker, the vision and optical products company with headquarters in New York, has a monthly peer recognition program to confer the Blue-Footed Booby Award to employees for high performance. The three winners choose prizes valued up to a few hundred dollars. An overall winner is selected quarterly, and the prize is travel to any city where the company is located.

> "Everyone wants to be appreciated, so if you appreciate someone, don't keep it a secret."
>
> —MARY KAY ASH

Each month at **Zappos**, the Las Vegas, Nevada–based online retailer, teams are given an extra $50 to reward a team member who went above and beyond. **Cisco**, the IT giant based in San Jose, California, gives each of its teams a Fun Fund, for activities to celebrate completed projects and meeting goals.

At **Great Plains Software** (a part of Microsoft Dynamics GP in Redmond, Washington) projects can last as long as nine months, so project leaders celebrate along the way with dinners, picnics, and other forms of informal recognition as they reach milestones. They also use a two-part bonus program to spur on project teams. Team members receive half the bonus when they hit the product's target release date, and the other half 90 days after the release, based on the performance of the product. At the conclusion of projects, the teams create a Friends List to recognize non-team members who supported them along the way. Friends receive gift certificates and thank-you letters.

Hilton Hotels from McLean, Virginia, gives its managers an annual Recognition Calendar featuring 365 no- and low-cost, easy-to-implement ideas to appreciate employees. The calendar includes reminders and tips for enterprise-wide, brand, and department recognition programs; best practices; important dates like International Housekeeping Week; and recognition quotes to share with workers. Users can add employee service anniversaries and download a PDF or import a file into their personal calendars.

Kimpton Hotels, headquartered in San Francisco, California, extends its recognition practices to employees' families. When a child of an employee makes a school honor roll, Kimpton inducts the child onto Bill's Honor Roll and gives the child a gift card as well.

5 More Ways to Have Fun Recognition

1. Give plastic hand clappers for people to "give themselves and others a big hand."

2. After meeting a major goal/initiative, have executives make breakfast for all hands.

3. Go out to celebrate achievements and anniversaries.

4. Play bingo by filling in a square each time your team completes a task/meets goal.

5. Shave your head when your team makes goal. If you're bald, paint your dome.

PART III

Team-
Oriented Fun

Most Fun at Work happens with others you work with as part of achieving ongoing work responsibilities as part of a team or department. This can also be an ad hoc group or task force dedicated to addressing a specific problem or opportunities in your company.

Applying fun in a group setting can include simple behaviors, such as starting group meetings with a simple fun activity or icebreaker and encouraging everyone to participate, or more formal team-building activities that let everyone interact with others who they may not normally work with on a daily basis. Again, our recommended approach is to try, debrief, learn from, and try again.

A group of people affords many more opportunities for having fun than work on your own or with just one other person. There is a greater variety of experience, age, backgrounds, personalities, and even cultures that can provide a richness and texture for your work group.

Fun is a way to bridge those differences of your group and create a common denominator, a common experience that helps to bind the group together to achieve their desired goals. As Victor Borge once observed, "laughter is the shortest distance between two people," and having fun together is sure to increase the amount of laughter that occurs in your groups!

Chapters in this section are "Virtual Work," "Games, Contests & Competitions," and "Team Building, Teams & Committees."

CHAPTER 6

Virtual Work

Everything is better in your PJs.

—ANONYMOUS

No part of work has changed more than the recent movement to work from home, driven by the worldwide coronavirus pandemic. Most every worker who could work from home was granted permission to do so, and employees and companies did the best they could to adjust to the new circumstances.

Even before the pandemic, however, there was a drastic shift toward employees working remotely. An analysis done by FlexJobs and Global Workplace Analytics found that in the five years prior, the number of employees working remotely increased 159 percent. International Workplace Group found 80 percent of U.S. workers say they would turn down a job that didn't offer flexible working, and more than a third said they would prioritize such arrangements over having a more prestigious role. In Crain's Future of Work survey, more than three-fourths of respondents cited flexible schedules and remote work as the most effective non-monetary ways to retain employees.

How does working virtually affect employees' fun and happiness? A study of 1,001 remote workers by Amerisleep found that they are 57 percent more likely than the average American to be satisfied with their job, plus, nearly 80 percent of respondents described their typical stress level during the workweek as either "not stressed" or only "moderately stressed." And another study by Owl Labs found that people who work remotely at least once a month are 24 percent more likely to be happy and productive.

Many organizations are finding creative ways to deliver fun experiences to their remote workers. And your efforts can go beyond popular videoconferencing platforms and apps such as Zoom, Webex, Google Meet, Slack, BuzzFeed, Houseparty, and so on. In this chapter we will look at specific examples of how virtual work can be made more fun.

Cynthia Burnham, a leadership coach, speaker, and author, encourages people to take pictures from around their houses, neighborhoods, and vacations to use as virtual backgrounds. She also suggests they "rename" themselves as someone inspiring, such as Colin the Brave or Susie, Empress of Tech. "This helps people get to know each other better, and also is fun!" says Burnham.

"My wife and I both work out of our home," says Michael Canic, president of **Making Strategy Happen**, based in Denver, Colorado. "I'm upstairs and she's downstairs. To keep things fun, several times a day I go downstairs or she comes upstairs for a 'kissing break.' Now, even hearing the footsteps of the other person brings a sense of anticipation and a smile to our faces."

During the pandemic Bob's wife Jennifer tunes in to a short weekly "dance party" at 2 p.m. on Fridays on Instagram. "It's high-energy and fun—the perfect pick-me-up to end the week!" she says.

Jill Boone, the assistant VP of European talent development for **Enterprise Holdings** in Surry, United Kingdom, keeps a tradition of getting individuals on her team to sign and send birthday cards to another team member. After COVID-19 forced everyone to work virtually, she adapted the practice to e-cards.

Wardrobe-themed Zoom meetings are popular at **Carfax**, the Centreville, Virginia–based vehicle report company. Daily themes include Camo Day, Wear Crazy Colors Day, and Favorite Hat Day. Fridays are reserved for Carfax Swag Day.

GitLab, a web-based repository management company from San Francisco, California, encourages its remote employees to spend a few hours every week taking coffee breaks together through a video call.

Education company **General Assembly**, headquartered in New York City, hosts a video chat room for workers to join in the morning for watercooler chat over coffee.

Synlogic Therapeutics, a Cambridge, Massachusetts, biotech, sends pancake-making kits to employees' homes and asks people to post pictures of their breakfasts. "We had pancakes in all flavors and shapes—from 'Star Wars' ships to coronaviruses," explains CEO Aoife Brennan.

Trello Software, a web-based list-making application company based in New York City, offers lunch to its virtual workforce. Each employee can expense up to

$25. Another New York City firm, **North 6th Agency**, provides a similar opportunity.

The Society of Human Resources Managers (SHRM) recommends the following tips to ensure effective happy hours:

- Keep them small or appoint a moderator to facilitate. Have agendas for larger groups.

- Stress comfort and ensure attendees are effectively lit.

- Keep outside noise to a minimum.

- Use the grid/gallery view on video-conferencing platforms so you can see everyone in equal-size boxes while people are talking.

- Use the visual cues on the platform to minimize people talking over each other.

- Be a good listener.

Happy hours that include dogs have become popularly known as "yappy hours." Having a happy hour in your bathrobe? **LaSalle**, the Chicago, Illinois–headquartered global real estate investment firm, calls it Spa & Sip Night.

"With the COVID-19 life changes, our school had to go to e-learning," says Laura Schmidt Brady, director of human resources for **Marburn Academy** in New Albany, Ohio. "I started virtual happy hours for our staff. I invited them to submit topics of conversation like 'What is the first thing you will do when this crisis is over?' 'If you could pick a song or movie title to

---

7 Fun Activities for Virtual Teams

1. Home tours
2. Family/pet intros
3. Happy and "yappy" (w/ dogs) hours
4. "Guess who's the baby" picture
5. Lip-sync challenge
6. Pictionary
7. Scavenger hunts

go with COVID what would it be?' It's been fun and engaging. About 20 percent of the staff participate each time, which seems perfect for a Google Meet. Folks are appreciative of being able to see faces over the age of 12," Brady adds.

DeliveringHappiness.com hosts DHCafe, a two-hour weekly meeting for workers to attend and "cwerk." "It's not the dirty dance move," says Sunny Grosso, culture chief, "but a co-work! It's a casual and fun place to pop in and ask a few questions or connect with the team or even just be on camera while working on something. The host works on a walking treadmill and makes the vibe fun. It helps us collaborate and have casual and often innovative and collaborative conversations about things we're working on remotely in our corners of the world."

There's magic in the air at **SkinCeuticals**, the New York City–based science-backed skin care brand of L'Oréal, the world's leading beauty company. With COVID-19 keeping workers at home, general manager Tina Fair came up with something unique to keep people together and things moving in the right direction. Fair brought in a virtual magician for the "happy hour" that kicked off the national sales meeting. "The tricks were amazing and the response so positive, I had to have him do our marketing team meeting," says Fair. "I loved the ability to be entertained and connect virtually."

Wai Poc, an executive coach at **UnleashedLeaders .com** in San Francisco, shares a fun virtual activity: Quickly Getting to Know Each Other Virtually (otherwise known as Virtual Speed Dating). Here's how it works:

- Seven questions are created before the activity starts.

- People are simultaneously and randomly paired up.

- Round 1: Pairs ask each other the same question, such as, "What's your earliest memory?"

- Round 2: A new pairing answers a new question.

- Continues for five more rounds.

---

5 Things to Send Remote Employees to Show You Care

1. "Snail" mail handwritten thank-you cards
2. Company swag—water bottles, T-shirts, logoed desk toys, hats
3. Gift cards
4. Food and snacks
5. Wellness resources/ equipment

According to Carol Cochran, the director of people and culture at **FlexJobs**, a job-search website based in Boulder, Colorado, "if one person works remotely, everyone is working remotely." Employees participate in regular, virtual non-work gatherings to compete in trivia games, exercise in yoga and belly dancing classes, and celebrate baby showers.

Karen Angeliatta, an Atlanta, Georgia–based consultant and trainer, is a big advocate of Kahoot!, the online tool for educators that turns polling questions into games. "Kahoot! lets us build a Word Cloud from answers to a question. We also use Slack to let attendees share articles, photos, joint activities, etc.," says Angeliatta. "We had concerns working from home, now we will have even more concerns returning to work. We desperately need to lighten things up to overcome the fears and tensions everyone has."

Employees at **Tripwire**, based in Portland, Oregon, hosted a virtual happy hour via Webex with the customer experience team that turned into a game of Pictionary. Sarah Holt, customer experience manager, shares five tools you can use to play virtual Pictionary:

- Whiteboard and dry erase pen

- Pen and paper

- MS Paint

- Adobe products

- Google products

The Product Development Electrification Engineering Division of **Ford Motor Company** invited its employees and their families to participate in an online talent show, to be held before an all-hands meeting. The closing act, an employee heavy metal rock band, wrote and performed their own song, which "brought down the house." Chief engineer Brett Hinds says, "The concert was a huge success and we received a lot of positive feedback."

Windy City Fieldhouse, a Chicago, Illinois, corporate event provider, specializes in virtual scavenger hunts. Employees form teams to hunt and compete for points. The company also provides virtual pub trivia, complete with a virtual emcee and team breakout rooms.

The culture committee at **FitSmallBusiness**, a New York City–based resource company for small businesses, creates and facilitates engagement events and employs a "people experience specialist," a role filled by Tsion McNichols. "We hold events at times that are comfortable for our people in different time zones," says McNichols. They play games that translate well over video calls, like bingo, spelling bees, and Pictionary.

At a recent happy hour at Las Vegas, Nevada, online retailer **Zappos**, the company's artist in residence created an art project for interested employees. "We sent out a materials list ahead of time—just a few simple things that anyone could find around their home—and during happy hour he taught us a really cool technique for making shadow puppets with paper and string," says Krissee Chasseur, brand aura research and development lead. "We asked everyone who was crafting along with us to activate their cameras and mics so people could follow along with their work."

> "When you have confidence, you can have a lot of fun. And when you have fun, you can do amazing things."
>
> —JOE NAMATH

Lansing, Michigan–headquartered **Liquid Web**, an online hosting company, asks employees to complete a questionnaire about their interests and personality. They are then matched with an employee from a different location. The two swap questionnaires, and based on the other person's answers, they paint or draw a small 4 × 4 piece of art for their new friend.

Merkle Inc., a performance marketing company based in Burbank, California, sent printable artwork to its workers to use for video conferencing backgrounds.

NPR reported that at least one example of video-conferencing "artwork" has gone viral. A company manager tried to set a background filter on her Zoom meeting, and it turned her into a picture of a potato. She didn't know how to fix it, so she spent the whole meeting as the "potato boss." She was a great sport about it and the perfect example of how making

3 WAYS HYATT HOTELS HAS FUN VIRTUALLY

Valerie Hope, regional director for talent development for Hyatt Hotels Corporation, manages a virtual team that does some fun things to stay connected:

1. **Celebration Buddy.** When they were able to meet in person, the team members put their names in a bowl and each person drew the name of someone who became his or her "celebration buddy" for the next 12 months. Over the year they would celebrate that person in ways that were important to them, learning about them, and surprising them in fun and creative ways.

2. **Virtual "Me" Page.** Valerie asked team members to use magazines during their online meeting to make a collage of "who they are." At the end of the call, everyone shared their creations on Skype, and photos were posted online in a shared folder.

3. **Praise Barrage.** When employees finally met in person, Valerie asked everyone to name three positive words that describe each person on the team and what they most appreciate and admire in working with that person. Then, in round-robin fashion, everyone shared the words they chose, giving context, and adding stories. Valerie captured the words shared about each person, tracking repetitious ones. She then fed the words into www.wordle.net, and a word art image was created from the words, with repeated words presented more dominantly. For the group's next gathering Valerie framed and presented each person's word art to them!

room for humor in a remote work environment lifted spirits and moved the whole team forward.

San Diego, California–based **2Connect**, a globally recognized presentation coaching and training firm, invites their employees and independent contractors to participate in online artwork and poetry happy hours, with a twist. Prior to the artwork party, each person picks a famous painting, sculpture, drawing, or photo. Then they each create their own versions of them, using any online or household items, including themselves. At the party, each one shares their new masterpiece. Prior to the poetry party, the firm selects a topic or subject and asks each person to write and send in two individual lines of prose. Then the entire list of lines is sent to everyone so they can put the lines together in any order to form a complete poem, which is recited at the party. "Finding ourselves instantly virtual because of COVID-19 gave us the chance to connect more frequently, so I wanted to take advantage of that," says Diane West, 2Connect founder and president. "We could check in on each other, potentially create a fun distraction from our day-to-day stresses, and tap into the creative brilliance of the team. Of course, all of the activities are voluntary, but the engagement has been tremendous. We look forward to continuing these well beyond the virus."

Workers at Irvine, California–based **SecureAuth Corporation**, a global identity security firm, take daily five-minute music breaks on Zoom. They get recurring calendar requests and reminders. They sign up to share a song; some have their children and families perform. Others play a meaningful song on Spotify. The leader in Buenos Aires set up a Slack channel for his team. "So far we've heard songs popular to our country in certain decades," says Nichole Devolites, senior manager of customer experience and advocacy. "We had one employee perform a song he wrote with an acoustic guitar; another employee's family sang with one of the daughters playing the ukulele, and another employee's 13-year-old daughter played Chopin on the piano."

One Friday a month, the customer support team at **Zapier**, the San Francisco, California–based app-connecting software firm, hosts a virtual dance party. The team selects a song from Spotify and asks employees to open Photo Booth to record a five-second video of their dance moves. Employees then upload the clip to GIPHY to convert it to a GIF. Finally, the team makes and posts a montage of it on Zapier's company-wide Slack channel. **Incubeta**, the marketing service company headquartered in Cape Town, South Africa, does something similar using Google Hangouts.

After going into COVID-19 lockdown, Los Angeles, California–based author **Libby Gill** created an online "writing sprint" group to replace meeting in her favorite coffee shop. "It's fun, interactive, and has a similar vibe to our real coffee shop," says Gill. They give each other feedback and their time is often spent as a focus group—on titles, word choice, content direction, and so on. "I've gotten such a great response from my beta group (three months along

CASE STUDY

HOW ENVOY GETS NEARLY 100 PERCENT
PARTICIPATION AT ITS VIRTUAL ALL-HANDS MEETINGS

Going fully remote during the pandemic required several adjustments for this workplace platform company in San Francisco, California, but they purposefully planned to maintain its important office traditions to continue delivering an excellent workplace experience.

Envoy anticipated that its all-hands meetings would be challenging to replicate remotely. However, thanks to the hard work from its Workplace Technology team, its hosts, and presenters, the company saw nearly 100 percent employee attendance. Feedback from employees was encouraging: the meetings seem organic, free-flowing, and not overly produced.

Envoy's Recipe for Success

1. Prep meeting:
   - Gather presentations one week in advance.
   - Have presenters attend a prep session one day before the meeting.
   - Review who will open and close the meeting; time needed for each presenter; transitions.
   - Review tips for virtual "presence"—where/how to stand/sit, how to speak.
   - Review tech devices to use and how to use tools on the virtual conference platform; check Wi-Fi.

2. Use a behind-the-scenes technician, and run a "remote pre-flight check":
   - Decide on music playlist and when to play songs.
   - Lock the presentation deck.

- Set Zoom (including host and cohost) settings.
- Anticipate possible logistical issues unique to meeting.
- Load slides, videos, and other content in separate browsers on their own machines.
- Set up a running clock to track time.
- Set up Chat or Slack to communicate with host(s).

3. Make it fun:
   - Ask attendees to wear favorite clothes, sunglasses, coolest hat or headwear.
   - Ask them to load a funny image or baby picture for their background.
   - Encourage them to use "chat."

4. Get an energetic, engaging host who will:
   - Facilitate great chitchat when people log on.
   - Add necessary, diplomatic, and "fun" commentary throughout the meeting.
   - Keep things on track.

Use a variety of hosts from meeting to meeting.

and still going strong), that I've decided to launch more groups."

Employees who own Peloton exercise bikes at **Amica Insurance**, headquartered in Lincoln, Rhode Island, go for rides together online.

Huge, a global digital company based in Brooklyn, New York, hosts virtual lunchtime runs. Employees then post videos of their runs in their neighborhoods for others to see. **Go Canvas**, the Reston, Virginia–based mobile-platform company, hosts "fitness bingo." Each square on the card lists a different activity such as "drop and give me 50" and "favorite yoga pose." **NowSecure**, a software company from Chicago, Illinois, set up a "quarantine step challenge."

Beyond exercise and wellness classes, many companies also provide opportunities for remote workers to learn and share ideas for food recipes, financial strategies, and personal growth. **CarGurus**, an East Cambridge, Massachusetts–based car-shopping website, has employees teach virtual classes such as Building Resiliency and Cooking at Home. Remote-working pioneer **Xerox Corporation** hosts online recipe exchanges. **NowSecure**, a software company headquartered in Chicago, Illinois, hosts virtual contests such as Best Video Cooking Demonstration and Best Use of Leftovers.

Boston, Massachusetts–based **Help Scout**, a global help-desk software provider, holds monthly themed Troop Talks via Zoom that bring together groups of 10 or more employees. The people operations leader chooses a theme, like a recipe party (sharing favorite recipes) or "bon-app-etite" (discussing must-have phone apps), for each conversation. A date is set, giving people time to prepare what to say. During the call, everyone takes turns sharing. On other occasions, employees share more about their daily lives and personalities by showing a video tour of their homes.

Motley Fool, the private financial and investing advice company based in Alexandria, Virginia, showed the virtual home tour video of the company's accounting manager, which revealed that even in March the family's Christmas tree was still up.

New York City–based **Vox Media** hosts a daily story time for families, courtesy of its parent employee resource group. CEO Jim Bankoff recently read stories to families. Across town at agencies **F+B New York** and **The Media Kitchen**, workers bring their children or a glass of wine to end-of-day check-ins. Digital media firm **Goodway Group**, located in Jenkintown, Pennsylvania, hosted a half-hour Family Fun Friday for employees with children.

Executives at **Innovid**, inventors of interactive objects embedded in video, host meetings with children on their laps or showing off their pets. During virtual lunches at **PubMatic**, the Redwood City, California–headquartered programmatic advertising firm, employees showcase pets and kids as they eat lunch together.

The **New York Times** advertising team held a "pet parade" for workers to share their pets. And the editorial team at New York City–based media and events firm **AdExchanger** also set up a #wfh-pets-and-kids channel populated by the office's dogs, cats, and children.

---

7 More Fun Activities for Virtual Teams

1. Dance party
2. Group poetry or song writing
3. Recipes and cooking classes
4. Video games
5. Book clubs
6. Yoga and meditation
7. Peloton bike riding

Inuvo, the advertising technology firm based in Little Rock, Arkansas, sends its employees a hand-illustrated portrait, card, and customized mug on their birthdays.

At **Aceable**, the Austin, Texas–based drivers' education and defensive driving company, employees' birthdays are highlighted on a Slack channel, giving everyone else the chance to share well-wishes and GIFs tailored to each celebrant's personal preferences.

Long before COVID-19, **Buffer**, the San Francisco–based firm, started hosting a great variety of "virtual watercoolers" to keep its workers connected in work and play, from GIFs in HipChat to theme days on Sqwiggle to supportive notes on I Done This, and even their own UP! apps. They also use Facebook Groups to share books and jokes, and Jawbone UP to track and share fitness efforts.

Global public brokerage giant **JLL**, headquartered in Chicago, Illinois, uses an app, Houseparty, and the whiteboard on Zoom to play games: Pictionary, Heads Up!, trivia, and How Well Do You Know Your Vice Presidents?

The **Novartis Institutes for BioMedical Research** in Cambridge, Massachusetts, offers its remote workers access to TIGNUM X, an app that helps enhance performance, wellness, and work-life balance.

Sydney, Australia–based **Atlassian** set up a Slack channel called #social-remote for various work and personal-related topics to help its virtual workforce thrive in the new work environment.

GitLab, headquartered in San Francisco, California, uses Slack to help employees connect, and in the #donut_be_strangers channel, team members have the option to be randomly paired up by a bot called Donut. They can also join the Random Room, a chat on Google Hangouts that is always open.

Team Building, a Covington, Washington, creative activity provider, uses a Slack app, Donut, to power its favorite channel, #Random-Mr-Rogers. "This translates into more positive work experiences and more fun too," said CEO Michael Alexis. "We call the channel #MrRogers because you are getting to know your virtual neighbors." At the start and end of each week, Donut automatically pairs people for 30-minute video calls. Although on work time, employees are encouraged to limit their topics to non-work items. "We've heard from our staff that these calls have helped them develop more meaningful friendships as they explore interests and commonalities outside of the office," Alexis added.

Boston, Massachusetts–based venture capital firm **Underscore** uses two apps: RemoteHQ, meeting software for screen sharing, note taking, and live video; and Clockwise, a Chrome plug-in to help people find time to work between the day's slate of virtual meetings. Underscore also uses an app that works with Slack, allowing people to give each other "virtual tacos" to acknowledge their help. The company is planning an office taco party to celebrate the person who has collected the most tacos.

Los Angeles, California–based **DISQO** created a Surviving COVID-19 Slack channel. "It's given us a fun opportunity to get to know one another even better, as people frequently share photos of their work-from-home coworkers: their children, pets and significant others," said Anthony Fabiano, manager of people. "On top of this, we've also been hosting virtual happy hours and lunches to ensure people have face time with each other outside of the context of meetings."

> "Telecommuting should no longer be viewed as a nice-to-have, optional perk mostly used by working moms. Remote work is a core business strategy today."
>
> —CALI WILLIAMS YOST

Employees at **Momenta Pharmaceuticals**, a Cambridge biotech developing drugs for immune system disorders, formed online "journal clubs" to discuss new research related to diseases the company is developing products for. And to better understand how the COVID-19 virus may affect patients in Momenta's clinical trials, the company hosts a weekly virtual conclave.

March, a software company based in Cambridge, Massachusetts, created a job called "remote work and inclusion manager" to ensure remote workers have a high quality of work life.

CHAPTER 7

Games, Contests & Competitions

*You can discover more about a person
in an hour of play than in a year of conversation.*

—PLATO

Playing games at work is both fun and productive, research shows. In a recent survey by TalentLMS, 87 percent of surveyed employees said game elements make them feel more socially connected and provide a sense of belonging at work, and Daria Lopukhina at Anadea reports 90 percent of employees said they are more productive when they engage in some form of gamification at work.

Research also suggests that even so-called microbreaks are beneficial. Researchers at Kansas State University studied 72 full-time employees from a variety of industries and found that those who spent 1 or 2 minutes during breaks in their day playing games such as Candy Crush on their phones reported being happier than their peers. The same study found that employees reported spending 22 minutes playing video games during an eight-hour workday.

Having some friendly competition at work can also increase both fun and productivity in the workgroup, with 50 percent of people reporting that they benefit from it.

Let's take a look at some examples of how companies have embraced games, contests, and competitions at work to make things more fun.

Grand Rapids, Michigan–based **Open Systems Technologies**, a talent locater, is home to worker paper-airplane contests. Founder Dan Behm says, "What's cool is that it gets all these different people from different areas of our company hanging out together, laughing, and coming up with these crazy ideas."

At **Hyland Software**, a Westlake, Ohio–headquartered company, CEO A. J. Hyland sends surprise emails to his workforce inviting them to join him in the atrium that afternoon for a paper-airplane flying contest. There are also plenty of after-hours activities like paintball and Hyland Hold 'Em tournaments with a top prize of $500.

> "Adults are babies with big bodies."
>
> —BOB PIKE

Pyramid Solutions, an automation software firm in Bingham Farms, Michigan, encourages employees to spontaneously break into Nerf gun battles whenever the need arises. "It's a fun way to de-stress at work that doesn't take intense physical activity or lengthy setup or cleanup," says one senior systems engineer. When new employees start work, they are given a Nerf gun and told, "You're gonna need this." Employees from **YouEarnedIt**, a flexible employee engagement software platform, based in Austin, Texas, combined their YouEarnedIt points to fund and launch a Nerf battle team-building exercise. For

30 minutes, the entire office became a battleground where strategy, collaboration, and out-of-the-box thinking meant the difference between life and (virtual) death.

Headquartered in Mankato, Minnesota, toy company **FUN.com** also hosts Nerf gun wars, as well as annual Mario Kart and rock-paper-scissors tournaments. They also have a dedicated game room. Employees at **Google** and **The Nerdery**, a Minneapolis/St. Paul–based tech company, are also known for their many Nerf gun battles.

> "The supreme accomplishment is to blur the line between work and play."
>
> —ARNOLD J. TOYNBEE

Hopper, a mobile-only travel booking app based in Montreal, Canada, awards a special trophy for the winner of its ugly holiday sweater competition. "Since we have a few different offices, we created a dedicated Slack channel to share photos of all the sweaters. The winner was awarded a special trophy," says Brianna Schneider, director of communications.

Fast Company, a New York–based progressive business media publisher, holds office-wide Jeopardy contests.

Sheetz, a gas station–convenience store chain based in Altoona, Pennsylvania, has Olympic-style sandwich-building competitions.

Lip-sync contests are very popular at **AOL**, the New York City–based online service provider. They also happen frequently at Austin, Texas–based **Bigcommerce**, an online firm, and across the state, in Abilene, at the **Funeral Directors Life Insurance** company.

6 Benefits of Play and Games at Work

1. Improve cognitive functions, hand-eye coordination, and motor skills
2. Reduce stress and increase adaptability
3. Encourage and help build the team
4. Boost morale and motivate employees
5. Attract and retain talent
6. Clarify strategy

One of the staples in the **Pinterest** office is their beloved foosball table in the back room where employees gather to talk, laugh, and eat. The table is worn and falling apart, but employees say that is part of what makes it so much fun. Playing foosball, while brainstorming or discussing projects, is encouraged by Pinterest. It boosts adrenaline and gets the creative thoughts going. They've "event named" various foosball plays, like the "jedmund," which is when someone makes a long, slow goal from across the table, or a "probasco" when a goalie fumbles the ball into their own goal. No Pinterest foosball game is complete without merciless trash talking and lots of laughter.

Employees at Manchester, England–based **Melbourne**, an IT server hosting company, are known for playing the company's many arcade games. CEO Daniel Keighron-Foster says, "It's a reward for hard work, rather than a replacement for it. The idea is to make it impossible for someone to want to leave."

As reported by a SnackNation blog, workers at **TINYpulse**, the employee engagement software firm located in Seattle, Washington, play two simple games called Werewolf and Eat Poop, You Cat. In the first game, players accuse each other of being a werewolf that has been killing villagers in their sleep. The second game is similar to telephone Pictionary.

All Star Directories, an online education service headquartered in Seattle, Washington, has a Mandatory Fun Committee that organizes several competitions throughout the year, including miniature golf, table tennis, and air hockey tournaments.

Nihal Parthasarathi, CEO and cofounder of **Course-Horse**, a New York City–based company that connects people with classes, wanted to create a team environment, and he decided games were the fastest way to bond. Every week, the team goes to Washington Square Park or Central Park to play lawn and board games, such as bocce, KanJam, Cards Against Humanity, and Settlers of Catan. "I've discovered the best way to connect personally with employees is through game play," says Parthasarathi. "It creates a fun environment and levels the playing field so we can just connect as people."

"**Baxter International** had two divisions located on different floors of their headquarters in Chicago, so people never had much chance to interact with each other," says Harry Kraemer, the company's former CEO. "We brainstormed an idea that would get everyone to go through other departments and since we had 18 departments, we focused on indoor miniature golf! Every department had to create a golfing obstacle and all employees had a chance to play. While you were visiting every department you had to list the names of a couple of people you met. Each department had to name their hole and they spent weeks planning what they'd do. We gave out awards for things like Hardest Hole and everyone loved it. More importantly, employees got to know people from all the departments, which subsequently made it easier to work together on projects, move people between departments, and retain employees. The activity was so popular we ended up repeating it every year."

When Harry became CEO of the company, they also started softball teams in which every division had a team and those who worked at corporate were called the Baxter Orphans, since they weren't part of any specific division. When international employees came to visit the headquarters, they got to play on the teams, which often meant having to learn the sport from other employees. This activity was also hugely popular and was repeated yearly, increasing the amount of camaraderie, communication, and fun among the company's 55,000 employees. They switched things up and sometimes had soccer games, which tended to give an edge to their European workers!

> "All work and no play makes Jack a dull boy."
>
> —JACK NICHOLSON

In another version of Baxter's team sporting events, they decided to play a game that no one had ever played before: Whirly Ball consisted of using bumper cars with a lacrosse stick to push and throw a ball into a basketball hoop. They'd hold an awards ceremony for the event, with awards such as Most Points Scored and Biggest Cheater, and found it all was more fun than any traditional company awards ceremony.

> "Winning is only half of it. Having fun is the other half."
>
> —BUM PHILLIPS

An online marketing and consumer acquisition platform developer, **Core Digital Media**, located in greater Los Angeles, California, offers an annual dodgeball and kickball tournament that's enthusiastically attended. **Greenvelope**, the online invitation and RSVP tracking company based in Seattle, Washington, hosts daily foosball tournaments. And ultimate frisbee is a popular lunchtime game for the "Bambooligans" who work for Lindon, Utah–based **Bamboo HR**.

The **Kimpton Ink48 Hotel** in New York City may be open for business 24/7/365, but their work-to-play ratio is just as robust. Whether it's impromptu dance parties, yoga breaks, ball games, or navigating through an obstacle course, anything goes when it comes to enjoying their time together.

Dan Para, CEO of **GCL**, a logistics company in Downers Grove, Illinois, loves games, golf, and gambling. So he had an office game room created with a 12-seat card table, complete with GCL logo. Every Friday afternoon dozens of folks show up for Texas Hold 'Em.

A talent management software firm, **ClearCompany**, located in Boston, Massachusetts, has a regular monthly game night featuring poker and Cards Against Humanity. **The Nerdery**, a Minneapolis/St. Paul–based tech company, encourages its people to play the Magic card game during the day.

HVAC.com, a Monroe, Ohio–based heating, ventilation, and air conditioning company, offers many competitions throughout the year, including an annual chili cook-off competition, Ping-Pong matches, foosball tournaments, and kickball. One notable event: The push-up competition—a personal challenge to gradually improve everyone's personal best. Over a 30-day period, contestants worked their way up to 50 push-ups. It got the whole office involved and worked so well that they added a sit-up challenge the following year.

"The difference between work and play is only a matter of attitude. Work, fully done, is play."

—**GERALD MAY**

CASE STUDY

PTC UNIVERSITY SWIMS WITH THE SHARKS FOR INNOVATIVE IDEAS

Want to innovate? Need to evolve your products or portfolio? There may be no better way than to invite the people in your organization to help you discover the opportunities. Not only can it yield great ideas, but it helps give everyone in the company a stake in the direction of the business. A few years ago, PTC University, the learning and development center for the PTC software firm based in Boston, kicked off a crowdsourced approach to idea generation and innovation that was loosely inspired by the TV show *Shark Tank*. In the show, entrepreneurs pitch their ideas to investors (or "sharks"). The best ideas earn an investment from one or more of the sharks. "In our version the executives are the sharks and everyone in our part of the business has a shot at pitching their best ideas—hoping to get them funded," says Adrian La Sala, who ran the innovation tournament and later presented the process in a session at a learning conference. "I thought there was no better time than a Shark Week to share the same presentation about that version of our ever-evolving, *Shark Tank*–inspired, innovation process."

The Process
The process is a two-phased approach called Ideation to Innovation.

The Ideation Community Phase
The first phase is an online community submission and voting process broken into three steps:

1. **Ideate:** Get entire community involved in submitting ideas on a community site.

2. **Refine:** Users optionally refine ideas, in case comments on their idea inspired them to evolve it. Panel of judges trims list to identify the most promising ideas.

3. **Vote:** The crowd votes on the remaining ideas, influencing the judges who make final decisions.

This phase generated over 200 ideas, decreased to about 80 for the Vote step. From those 80, judges identified 20 ideas they wanted developed further in the next phase.

The Innovation Summit Phase

This phase focuses on its culmination—a live meeting loosely modeled on the TV show:

1. **Develop:** Presenters convert their ideas into "pitches" and are encouraged to involve colleagues in practicing and evolving their ideas.

2. **Pitch:** Ideas are presented or pitched live—in a fun format with strict time limits—eight minutes to present and five minutes for Q&A from the judges.

Judges use play money to invest in the ideas. And those ideas that prove the most promising are implemented.

The Results

"I product managed an idea that won in the first year," says La Sala. "That product launch may have had the largest impact of any before it at PTC University and as a result we have been using this process in some form or another to generate ideas and new innovations ever since."

However, the results are not only seen in the good ideas that are brought to market. Another result is an engaged organization. There are few chances in large organizations for every member to have a shot to have their ideas heard in front of executives. This process lets the best idea win.

With over 200 ideas submitted and hundreds of badges earned, it's safe to say the community rallied around this opportunity and embraced it. "Personally," adds La Sala, "I have also had an idea selected and implemented and can vouch that it was an engaging process, great opportunity, and wonderful learning experience."

continues on next page

The Approach

Like any community event, a large-scale event like this takes planning and orchestration. Keeping the process running, communicating the current status, and evaluating ideas and submissions all take people and time. Three overall plans are needed:

- **Process Plan:** The phases and stages described above, along with a timeline

- **Communication Plan:** The methods, messages, and imagery to communicate throughout the process

- **Recognition Plan:** The badges, awards, and leader boards to encourage and recognize participants

The Technology

In a large company you will need technology to make a tournament like this practical. You need a system that enables your team to submit ideas, comment on ideas, and vote on ideas. Additionally, having a system that supports communication, recognition, and judging helps too.

There is a free online tool—the Darwinator—that can run your own innovation tournament. The authors of that tool are also the authors of a book you'll find on their site, darwinator.com.

Riot Games, maker of League of Legends video games, has a "play fund" where "Rioters" can spend up to $300 per year on other video games.

Progressive Insurance, headquartered in Mayfield, Ohio, holds an artificial intelligence competition for their employees.

> "There is no real difference between work and play—it's all living."
>
> **—RICHARD BRANSON**

For over a decade, **The Container Store**, a storage and organization company based in Coppell, Texas, has held its annual Soap Box Derby. The event features cars and costumes. At one recent event, the DC Transportation team donned 1940s zoot suits and drove their *Godfather* car. The Marketing team piloted the *Magic School Bus* car, and Merchandising wore lab coats as they jumped in their *Jurassic Park* car, with a T-rex in tow.

London, United Kingdom, company **Pricewater-houseCoopers**, the audit and consulting firm, hosts annual international sports tournaments in soccer and basketball for its global employees.

William Pickens, owner of **Pool Covers Inc.**, in Fairfield, California, often hangs a number on the wall and rewards employees who know how it is related to the business. For example, 22.5 is the average miles per gallon of the delivery truck fleet, and those who knew it received a $10 prize. Pickens says this game gets employees to think about the business and also creates camaraderie.

The Fun Committee at **Iteris Inc.**, a provider of solutions to the traffic management market, sponsored a

Guess the Stock Price on March 31 contest, in which the winner got a free lunch at a local restaurant. The company also launched Project Girth. For every pound an employee lost, a dollar would be sent to his or her favorite charity.

***

Distractions are common in the workplace, but employees at **Nationwide Insurance** in Columbus, Ohio, have a secret weapon: hours of computer time spent balancing a virtual basketball while other objects fly across the computer screen. Nationwide encourages workers to play this game, among others, and has made it a part of its wellness plan. The games teach concentration and stress management techniques to boost function and memory and increase positive thinking.

***

Nugget Markets, a Woodland, California–based upscale supermarket chain, has an annual Bag-Off Championship, where courtesy clerks vie for the Best Bagger title.

***

John Petrusa, founder of **People Business Solutions Inc**. in Wheaton, Illinois, shares the story of his client, **Hursthouse Landscape Architects**, a design/build landscape company based in Bolingbrook, Illinois, that was having difficulty getting work crews to be efficient leaving the yard in the morning and promptly getting to the work sites. His firm designed a "tote board" in the equipment barn and identified the employees in the five work crews, including the supervisors' names.

---

5 Fun Play Ideas to Try at Work

1. Paper-airplane flying contest
2. Hockey in the hallways
3. Nerf-gun fight around workstations
4. Water-gun fight in parking lot or CEO's office
5. Remote-control car race—indoors or out

"We then created a friendly competition between crews that included quality metrics as well as speed and budget parameters," he explains. "Every Monday morning at 7 a.m., the leadership team would identify the team scores from the previous week and the team with the most 'points' would move their team's token ahead on the tote board. At the end of each month, the team in the lead would receive a cash bonus. The team leader would come forward and be given a $100 bill and each team member $50.

"In addition to the cash bonus program, the company created a friendly competition in the yard during poor weather days. Team members would compete while demonstrating basic hardscaping techniques. This time was also used to give practice time and coaching to crew members to develop or improve their hardscaping skills."

> "My childhood may be over, but that doesn't mean playtime is."
>
> **—RON OLSON**

At **Four Pi Systems**, a developer of manufacturing test equipment in San Diego that is now a part of **Hewlett-Packard**, the internal Applications Team was the first group to install and test software. They often became frustrated when they found bugs in the software, so the software development team started a Find a Bug, Win a Buck program that awarded a dollar-bill to anyone who found a bug in the new software product. The program changed people's attitudes and improved software quality because more bugs were reported and fixed sooner.

> "If you're not really having fun then there's no point of really trying."
>
> **—WILLOW SMITH**

A competition was designed for four **Deloitte** (a professional service firm) offices in India, to boost engagement and promote innovation and entrepreneurship. Employees were invited to join teams and develop solutions to real-life business problems. The program was called Maverick, and teams were judged based on their ability to identify critical issues of their own choice and develop solutions. The competition was designed to be playful. The program was formatted like a reality show where a team was eliminated every week, while winning teams advanced. Winners received small financial rewards and the chance to work with senior leaders on projects such as branding exercises.

Hardee's Food Systems, the fast-food chain headquartered in St. Louis, Missouri, held a Competition for Excellence, in which three-person teams from each of more than 2,000 restaurants competed against other Hardee's restaurants in their districts. Regional managers judged the teams on four basic qualifications for fast-food employees: (1) service, (2) product makeup, (3) work area cleanliness, and (4) how well they worked together. Winning teams advanced to the regional competition, and seven finalists were flown to the company's headquarters. Cash awards were given at each level, with the winners of the national competition receiving $1,500 per team member. All the national finalists were flown on the company jet, whisked around the city by limousine, and treated like VIPs.

Greene Turtle restaurants in the Tri-State and New York area host annual competitions among bartenders—from within and outside of the company—to create new and exciting cocktails. Bartenders submit their concoctions, and the winners are added to an updated drink menu.

To identify and develop promising talent, the **Hyatt Hotels** chain, headquartered in Chicago, Illinois, sponsored an in-house cooking competition called The Good Taste Series. Every hotel could submit one contestant. Six finalists won two rounds of competition, against more than 220 colleagues from Hyatt hotels in 40 countries, for the chance to compete globally. All chefs below the executive chef level were eligible to participate. In the Americas region alone, there were 12 regional competitions with 12 to 15 competitors each. Regional winners received $2,000 cash and an all-expenses-paid trip to the finals in Singapore, where they competed for a $3,000 cash prize. The series was run *Iron Chef* style, with chefs given a black box of secret ingredients, and two days to prepare two dishes for a panel of judges.

At many of **Amazon**'s warehouses, workers spend company time playing video games. Some race virtual dragons or sports cars around a track, while others collaborate to build castles piece by piece. They race to fill customer orders, with progress reflected in a video game format. Games are displayed on small screens at employees' workstations. As robots wheel giant shelves up to each workstation, lights or screens indicate which item the worker needs to put into a bin. The games can track tasks and can pit individuals, teams, or entire floors in a race to pick or stow various items. Game-playing employees are

> ### 5 More Fun Play Ideas to Try at Work
>
> 1. Office Olympic events using swivel chairs and other equipment
> 2. Desk chair races (backward)
> 3. Impromptu rubber-band wars
> 4. Trivia night with questions about company products and services
> 5. Human bowling tourney: strap people to skateboards and push toward Skittle candies (pins) at end of parking lot

rewarded with points and virtual badges throughout their shifts.

Uber and **Lyft**, both ride-sharing companies based in San Francisco, California, use gamification to keep drivers on the road longer. They give cash rewards for completing goals such as 60 rides in a week or 20 more miles.

Target, a Minneapolis, Minnesota–based retail company, has used games to encourage cashiers to scan products more quickly, and **Delta Air Lines**, an airline company with headquarters in Atlanta, Georgia, used games to help train reservation agents. "This is most successful when the games are replacing tasks that are otherwise boring," says Gabe Zichermann, a gamification consultant. "Anything to reduce the drudgery, even the smallest amount, is going to give a bump to workers' happiness."

Ms. Sim Siew Gek, executive administrator for **Amplus Communication Pte Ltd** in Singapore, says: "I totally agree with the concept of having more fun at work! Even for adults, I strongly believe that if you want to drive an idea into the group, including an element of fun works wonders. We have about 50 office staff and another 50 rank and file in the production line. We have a diversity of manpower, including different races from different countries. For several years, my HR department was not given any budget to run any 'morale' programs, so we had to craft out ideas for events that cost next to nothing. One particular year, to celebrate Singapore's National Day, we devised a game to involve as many staff as possible. Our objective was (1) give opportunity for staff of different ranks to team up and get to know each other, and (2) learning about our country history and culture.

"Teams were set up, with the criteria that each team needed to be comprised of participants from different departments. Team members were despatched to participate in different levels of games. One game tested agility skills, another asked intellectual questions, and another was a challenge for speed, like a large picture puzzle. The game lasted one and a half hours. It created fun and excitement, and it also kick-started team spirit as it requires cooperation and encouragement from each other. The event was a much talked-about topic during lunch breaks as staff teased each other about how silly each of them were and the overall fun they had."

CHAPTER 8

Team Building, Teams & Committees

Where people aren't having fun, they seldom produce good work.
—**DAVID OGILVY**

Another fun and valuable social activity at work is team-building activity, which helps to build rapport among team members or across the organization, making it easier to communicate, collaborate, and get work done. It also helps to create an organization that has greater loyalty, a greater ability for employees to move within the organization, and increased employee retention.

Queens University of Charlotte found about 75 percent of employers rate teamwork and collaboration as "very important," yet only 18 percent of employees get evaluated on those elements in their performance reviews. They also found that 39 percent of surveyed employees believe that people in their own organization don't collaborate enough. And some 86 percent of employees and executives cite lack of collaboration or ineffective communication for workplace failures, a Fierce Inc. survey found.

The same study also found 49 percent of Millennials support social tools for workplace collaboration and would even be willing to pay out of pocket for social collaboration tools to improve productivity.

According to an Alfresco survey of more than 753 business professionals, it was found that nearly 83 percent of professionals depend on technology to collaborate.

Mercer found 33 percent of employees say the ability to collaborate makes them more loyal, and Gust found 37 percent of employees say "working with a great team" is their primary reason for staying at a job.

Let's look at some examples of how companies better promote team building and collaboration in their companies, which allows for more fun for everyone involved.

At Ada Township, Michigan—based **Amway**, the world's largest direct-selling company, employees are encouraged to help each other out. On days when workloads are light in a particular department, employees help workers in other departments. After accumulating eight hours of working in other departments, employees receive a thank-you note from the vice president of corporate relations. Additional time earns employees a luncheon with company executives.

Because he tends to charge through obstacles, Michael Gladysz, the team leader with **Huntington National Bank** in Akron, Ohio, started calling himself The Gladiator. "When Robbie, who loves seafood, got a huge sunburn, we decided he would be The Robster," says Gladysz. Now, nearly everyone in the office has a nickname, and the bank's graphic designer created avatars for everyone based on their nicknames. "It's made us all feel like we are a stronger part of the Team," adds Gladysz.

Don Coyhis describes how a humor seminar helped when he was district manager for **Digital Equipment Corporation**'s Colorado customer support center: "We taught everyone to juggle bean bags; if employees felt uptight after a call, they were encouraged to juggle to break the tension and prepare for the next call. We also instituted a 'grouch patrol' to tell grouchy people to take a break. We found that if we systematically took breaks, productivity improved."

Where common understanding and alignment were needed to set up vision and mission elements, Stella Ioannidou, IT workforce management unit supervisor for **Eurobank** in Greece, did it through a Lego Serious Play workshop. She also notes that her team abides by the Scrum playbook, making work both efficient *and* fun because they engage in so many meaningful conversations that make people feel at ease and de-stressed during work. "Increased efficiency allows us time to be nice and lively *because* we have efficient structures and tools in place to take our minds off the nitty-gritty," she explains.

There is an Innovation Lab at **AdventHealth** in Orlando, Florida. When employees need to identify an improvement process, or are faced with a management problem, they can present their issues to the team in the lab. People from different departments meet to discuss ways to solve the issues. The team offers Wisdom Wednesdays, when they host lunch and a 30-minute discussion of an issue. Sometimes they have a TED talk–like presentation. "My partner and I presented 'What else is inside of you?'" says employee Laura Gerow. "I write short stories so I read a few and my songwriting partner talked about writing songs and then we presented our new song to them. It was one of the highlights of my life since I had never presented anything to an audience before. We all have so much fun and it's amazing what you can do in 30 minutes."

When Mario led the collaborative organizational design team at **The Ken Blanchard Companies**, based in Escondido, California, the team needed a break from the several-months-long process. The team took to the shores of Mission Bay in San Diego to debrief its activities over seafood and a few brews. Each dedicated member then shared their best moments of the process, and they all laughed heartily as they made a bonfire from the many flip-charts from their sessions. It was a welcome relief that renewed their energies for the last few months of the venture.

Warby Parker, the New York City–based prescription glasses retailer, fields an employee Culture Team that organizes company outings, themed luncheons, and other events. One example: To encourage collaboration among the staff, the team selects random workers to have lunch together. A part of the hiring process, the team also helps ensure their desired culture continues as the company grows.

CASE STUDY

ATLASSIAN SOFTWARE GOES ALL OUT IN THE 24 HOURS OF SHIPIT

This Sydney, Australia–headquartered global firm hosts a 24-hour hack-athon called ShipIt. Workers (Atlassians) from every department and level participate—from new hires to the C-suite—dropping their current work to create something innovative. They form ad hoc teams to collaborate with people they don't usually work with in order to work on ideas, from engineering and design, to legal and finance. Projects can be technical or nontechnical, of any shape and size, applicable to small teams or to the entire company. And there are few rules, to encourage the teams to work on whatever they wish.

Past initiatives include the following:

- Identifying ethically sourced clothing for the Atlassian Foundation

- Creating expat guides for newly transferred Atlassians

- Enabling customers to pay for cloud products via PayPal; and Jira Service Desk

When the company launched ShipIt, 14 developers participated in one location. Years later, nearly 4,000 Atlassians participated across more than 20 cities in over 11 countries. As the hackathon has grown, it has also evolved. "You might even say we've innovated on the innovation contest," say blog authors Dominic Price and Philip Bradock. For example, they started an entirely virtual ShipIt for the increasing size of their remote workforce. "We've also introduced a Customer Kick-Ass Prize, where an Atlassian customer picks a winning project that delivers clear value," the authors add.

ShipIt builds camaraderie across the company and injects creativity into its products, operations, and processes. And many Atlassians regard ShipIt as their "24 hours of opportunity."

At Salt Lake City, Utah–based **OC Tanner**, an employee engagement and recognition firm, workers are asked to bring an idea, news story, or article to the Monday team meeting. The firm encourages its workers to pull information from any reputable source. In the meeting, employees share their idea or article and how the information could create a positive (preferred) or negative impact on the business, employees, or clients. "It offers great insights and makes for lively conversation and engagement. Importantly, it offers interesting business related and entertaining topics while welcoming different perspectives," says Mike Bruce, managing director of client solutions.

Sparks, a Philadelphia, Pennsylvania–based global brand-experience agency, runs a program called Mix and Mingle where workers are chosen from different departments to get to know each other over lunch. In Santa Monica, California, **Genly**, a marketing and advertising firm, offers biweekly company lunches. "It's great because it gives me the chance to get to know the co-workers that I don't work with on a daily basis," says one employee. "We do a lot of really fun company outings such as a very cool Star Wars VR experience."

> "If I quit having fun, then it's time for me to quit working."
>
> —**CHARLAINE HARRIS**

Meissner-Jacquet, the San Diego, California–based commercial real estate firm, treated all of its workers to a day of team building at the San Diego Zoo. After cocktails and a gourmet lunch, they had a trivia quiz, followed by the main event—a scavenger hunt. Chief spiritual officer and HR business partner Angela Robertson formed five teams so that each team had people from different departments. The main task: visit and bring back photographs of the animals. The challenge: it was an extremely hot day and most animals took to the shade, out of view of humans. "They [teams] really had to get creative," says Robertson. One team went to the gift shop and took pictures of the stuffed animals. "They broke the rules. But, everyone had a lot of fun. It was nice to get out of the office and work with people you don't get to normally and not have to follow rules exactly," adds Robertson. "And our newest employee had her best ever first week on the job."

"Things were getting especially stressful for my leadership team," says Tina Fair, general manager of **SkinCeuticals**, the science-backed skin care brand of **L'Oreal**, the world's leading beauty company. "And, 'battling it out' was exactly what they needed." So, for its next off-site meeting, Fair reserved a boxing ring at a Manhattan gym, and the team engaged in some fun, friendly sparring. "My team is located all over the country. Getting together at these offsites is huge," says Fair. "These tone-setting activities are critical for us to continue to collaborate and support each other. And the boxing renewed our team spirit and fighting mode. I absolutely love my team!"

Penguin Random House, a book publisher located in New York, encourages team building by allowing employees to form or join book clubs with colleagues to meet and discuss books. The company incentivizes worker participation by offering its Free Books Program. Workers can order multiple books and e-books, free of charge, from a list of more than 100 titles, which is updated throughout the year. Likewise, **MyEmployees**, a management consulting company based in Castle Hayne, North Carolina, has a weekly one-hour book club meeting. They discuss personal development books about motivation, financial discipline, stress management, and interpersonal relationship development.

Poppin is an office supply company based in New York City that offers products with bold modern design. Its mission is "Work happy." The Nifty Fifty program encourages employees to get to know one another and hang out. The program reimburses employees up to $50 for doing something fun outside the office, like going to a concert or getting a manicure.

> "No one can whistle a symphony. It takes a whole orchestra to play it."
> —H. E. LUCCOCK

When Cynthia Alt was vice president of organization development at **Banker's Trust**, she organized a miniature golf course for a senior leader who was a big golfer. Each department produced a creative and elaborate mini-golf hole. Foursomes were made up of two people from one department and two people from another department. They rented clubs and balls from a mini-golf course for two hours for $20. The activity was so successful, the company offered it three years in a row. Alt, now a professor at USC, also hosted an Easter egg hunt. Everyone was asked to hide a plastic egg with the name of a randomly selected coworker inside. "If you found someone else's egg, you could re-hide it. And some had clues to find other eggs. The game went on for two days," says Alt.

---

10 Fun Team-Building Ideas

1. Create a Fun Committee and rotate membership.
2. Ask team to make top-10 list of funniest things that occurred at work that week.
3. Plan a volunteer outing with a charity like Habitat for Humanity.
4. Take team to a painting or sculpture class.
5. Take team to a cooking class.
6. Ask team to paint an inspirational mural on a wall.
7. Take team scavenger hunting.
8. Take workers go-carting.
9. Form book club and buy books for members.
10. Rent a pool hall and host department tourney.

Recently hired Melissa Haas, office manager at **Mannix Marketing**, was excited to bring new ideas to the company and promote deeper friendships. Because the Winter Olympics were that year, Haas took advantage of the hype and created the Mannix Marketing Office Olympics. She split the company into three countries (teams) and assigned each a color. Each team chose a "king" who served as their captain. Country names were Blue Steel, Green Acres, and Scarlet Fever. Everyone received a bandana in their country's color so they could show their team spirit over the upcoming two weeks. Because the event was relatively complex, Haas engaged a friend and coworker to help out. "Everyone had a blast competing," says Haas.

Day 1. Opening Ceremony. Pizza party kickoff and trivia using Easy Buttons from Staples

Day 2. Paper Wad Basketball

Day 3. Kitchen Challenge. Players ate baby food, immediately followed by a stack of crackers, then tried to whistle.

Day 4. Coffee Stair Race. People timed how fast they could go up stairway with mug of water.

Day 5. Grammar Contest

Day 6. Postponed because of snow

Day 7. Trivia Game

Day 8. (Part 1) Typing Test

Day 8. (Part 2) Make up for snow day. Worst Website (identify and submit to third-party judge)

Day 9. Graphic Design Contest. Create hybrid of a leader and head of a weird-looking ostrich.

Day 10. Get-Out-of-the-Beanbags and into Wheel Barrel Race. Bonus: Office Pranks Contest

Day 11. Final Ceremonies. Chili Cook-Off. Variations included vegetarian, spicy, and venison.

After finishing the Office Olympics, the company held a Wii bowling tournament.

Canon Solutions America in Norcross, Georgia, sends a cart ladened with ice cream, Popsicles, and water around its offices to serve teammates. What's unique is the traditional ice-cream-truck music playing from the cart.

Kevin Sheridan, former president of **HR Solutions** and author of *Building a Magnetic Culture*, planned many team outings throughout the year. For example, taking his team to Millennium Park for ice cream treats. Often on Fridays, they all go to the movies for three hours. And once a month, they'll take two hours off to play a game.

Three times a year, employees at **Hubspot**, an inbound marketing software firm based in Cambridge, Massachusetts, attend a mystery dinner. No one knows where they are going to eat or with whom until 4 p.m. the day of the event.

PLAE, a custom children's footwear company based in San Francisco, California, hosts a quarterly cooking "team-building" retreat. Two teams of on-site workers compete in an "ironless" chef cook-off using only office tools. Remote employees call in to rank each dish on presentation and story. In another competition, teams made "a fancy birthday cake entirely from doughnuts," says e-commerce VP Jeff Ha. Company cofounders consider the events morale boosters and "a welcome distraction from the daily grind."

> "If you want to go fast, go alone. If you want to go far, go together."
> —AFRICAN PROVERB

The Expert Services Team at **Mendix**, the Boston, Massachusetts–based app development firm, meets weekly at a Beer & Learn session. Each member gives an update of their work; what, if any, obstacles they experienced; and what is occurring the following week. Then, to mentor the rest of the team, one member shares a learning. "We want to encourage each team member to not only take the time to learn something new each week but also to share the learning with the rest of the team," says company vice president Donna Williams. "This aspect of the meeting instills the importance that improving individually subsequently benefits and strengthens the team's collective expertise."

When Brad Zehner was president of **Worldwide Marketing and Sales**, a conglomerate of 12 different machinery companies located in six countries, he had the challenge of integrating several marketing and sales units. "Whenever we had a meeting of the 'troops,' we always had 'Fun Times,' which among other topics, singled out one colleague in some fun way. We always selected individuals who could laugh at themselves since we never wanted to hurt anyone's feelings," Brad says.

"One of the most successful 'Fun Times' was a U.S. meeting of sales engineers. We had one guy who covered the Carolinas and Georgia who was absolutely addicted to peanuts. While driving, he would crack and eat peanuts. The floor of his car was awash in peanut shells like the bars which encourage you to throw your peanut shells on the floor. If he had to take a potential customer to lunch or dinner, he would vacuum his car, which smelled like a big jar of peanut butter. All his peers would frequently josh him with nicknames such as 'Mr. Peanut Man,' 'Peanut Butter,' 'the Nut,' 'Pee Wee,' etc. about his 'peanut addiction,' which he jovially acknowledged.

"At the sales meeting, Peanut Man was invited by his sales manager to come on stage for a 'special and unique' award. After appropriate comments about his contributions to our organization's successes, etc. his sales manager signaled a forklift driver off stage to come on stage. On the forklift was not one, but two, huge 500-pound bags of peanuts. His peers just roared with laughter as did he. Within 24 hours, everyone worldwide heard of Peanut Man's special award. After the meeting, we had the two 500-pound bags shipped to his home. His wife mandated the bags be stored in the garage!"

On occasion, the leadership team at **AdventHealth** in Orlando, Florida, would go out as a group to do volunteer work. "We painted one of the habitats at our zoo in Sanford, and returned later to help out with their big Easter egg hunt," says Laura Gerow. "Then we had lunch and roamed the zoo." Gerow set

10 More Fun Team-Building Ideas

1. Invite workers over to watch significant event on the big screen.
2. Take team to improv comedy.
3. Host a BBQ at your home with games like three-legged races.
4. Have a pool party at manager's house with potluck dinner.
5. Host bowling event.
6. Plan a float/rafting trip down a local river.
7. Hire team-building company to customize team event.
8. Get personal-preference expert to facilitate a team experience.
9. Rotate team members to facilitate team meetings.
10. Rent seating section at sporting event for team and significant others.

up a two-day, overnight team-building excursion at Camp Wewa in Apopka, where her son was the director. "We had so much fun, I very much encourage teams to do this at local camps." The company also set up a Christmas event featuring a scenic boat ride in Winter Park, then a visit to the Morse Museum, followed by lunch at the Hidden Gardens restaurant. About 90 percent of the people said they had never done any of that before. "Great day. I believe this has brought the leadership team so much closer. As far as my little team of executive assistants we have a lot of fun up here. We laugh a lot and have potlucks, and do volunteer work two or three times a year. Everyone helps when you are in need."

> "Individual talent can win games. Focused, disciplined teamwork wins championships."
> **—ANONYMOUS**

General Mills has a Spirit Team that hosts between eight and ten team-building events annually, like Volunteer Days where employees volunteer at nonprofit organizations. Positive feedback from employee surveys cites a connection between the volunteer program and good feelings about their jobs as well as the company.

> "I think the next best thing to solving a problem is finding some humor in it."
> **—FRANK A. CLARK**

Teamwork is a key company value at **VideoAmp**, the video advertising optimization firm headquartered in Santa Monica, California. The company demonstrates this value through regularly hosted fitness challenges. Senior manager of talent Julia Saidnia says, "Employees team up across all of their locations and the majority participate in fitness challenges, which promote internal networking across all levels. These team-building exercises are what inspire us to get in shape together."

LinkedIn, the online employment-oriented service firm from Sunnyvale, California, partnered with **Adventure Architects**, a San Francisco–based corporate retreat experience firm, to challenge executives at a ski resort in the Sierra Nevada mountains. Employees were awakened early morning with a frantic knock on the door. They were instructed to organize a high-stakes search-and-rescue mission for a fictional missing skier and were given maps, compasses, and avalanche beacons, among other equipment. Then during a fireside chat, their performance was debriefed by an executive coach. "Teams connect when they are having fun and genuinely challenged," says company founder Noah Rainey.

The Go Game, an interactive team-building production company headquartered in San Francisco, is especially known for producing a very popular scavenger hunt. Other activities include espionage-themed adventure games, music video competitions, and a Go gameshow.

Shutterstock, a stock photography business located in New York, hosts an annual 24-hour hackathon, where employees compete for prizes and a chance to have their projects officially funded and launched by the company.

PART IV

Organization-Oriented Fun

Ultimately, fun works best when it is openly encouraged throughout the organization and becomes an expected and anticipated part of everyone's role and experience at work. This doesn't tend to happen by accident, but rather from a systematic application and appreciation of the topic by a significant portion of its members.

Ideally, top management would encourage and support fun in the work environment, even participating in the process. But creating a fun-oriented organization does not have to be dependent solely on its senior leaders.

For example, an easy starting point is to create a Fun Committee that is represented by individuals from a cross section of your organization (including an executive "sponsor") to brainstorm, prioritize, and implement fun activities on an ongoing basis.

We'll examine general working conditions, down to specific categories, and how to make traditional office celebrations and events more fun for everyone.

A critical mass of employees focused on fun activities can help to shape the culture of the organization over time until it becomes an accepted and embedded part of "how we do things around here." Some organizations even go so far as to list Fun as one of their core behavioral values that the organization aspires to have as an integral part of how it chooses to function and a cornerstone of the organization's success.

CHAPTER 9

Working Conditions

Life is better when you're laughing.

—ANONYMOUS

Another easy, yet important way to affect the level of fun at work is by paying attention to employee working conditions.

For example, a report by CMI Workplace found that if workers feel happy in their office surroundings, they are less likely to be stressed at work. This is especially relevant given that more than half of Americans report exposure to unpleasant and potentially hazardous working conditions and nearly one in five American workers are exposed to a hostile or threatening social environment at work, according to the American Working Conditions Survey.

You can make your company's working conditions an asset and advantage for your employees. Let's look at some examples of how companies are doing that today.

Relationship-driven leadership consulting firm **Skye-Team**, based in Broomfield, Colorado, doesn't just tell its staff that working with the firm will be fun. They mean it. To help its stakeholders to remember, expect, and demonstrate fun, four of their eight core values are "Have fun." Founder and CEO Morag Barrett says, "Having fun is infectious. It immediately breaks down barriers and connects people—clients and associates. When we share experiences and enjoy each other, it's easier to figure out the real problems and the best solutions." CSO Ruby Vesely, who has been known to dress up in a Kiss rock band costume, considers the whole team personal friends. "I don't get up in the morning to work for myself, I work for us, our families, each other." COO Eric Spencer agrees. Spencer recently designed and delivered a safety program for the oil and gas industry. He feels his genuine and friendly banter before and during sessions helped to build trust with his groups. The result: the client experienced a 17 percent drop in safety problems. "We show up as ourselves. We're authentic, prepared, we listen, and have fun. And get great results," says Spencer.

Perkins Coie, a Seattle, Washington–headquartered law firm, celebrated its 100th anniversary by giving every employee a book of the firm's history. They also give awards based on candy bars (Nestlé Crunch bar for "You helped me out in a crunch!" and a PowerBar for "You really helped us power through"). An anonymous Happiness Committee also leaves gifts at workstations.

> "We believe in working hard and having fun at the same time. It's a way of life for me, and I feel tremendous."
>
> —ROBERT STIGWOOD

LEGO, the plastic brick toy company based in Billund, Denmark, promotes a "growth" culture, which means there is no company handbook on what people can and cannot do. This gives workers the chance to unleash their imagination and creativity in their day-to-day lives, and it shows the company's core values of fun and laughter.

No company handbook? How about no formal job roles? **Aviture**, the Omaha, Nebraska–based research, competitive analysis, and software development company, hires people with no specific role in mind. In an approach called "butterflying," managers develop employees' jobs as they go. The roles are fluid—people can rotate to other roles and customize job responsibilities toward work they want to do. The organizational structure is relatively flat, and executive leadership is easily accessible to any employee. It's as easy as knocking on the door or scheduling a lunch.

Cybersecurity awareness training company **KnowBe4**, based in Clearwater, Florida, has a very lax dress code. CEO Stu Sjouwerman is known for saying, "If what you're wearing doesn't get you arrested on the way to work, you're good."

When noted author and celebrated raconteur Peter Jensen was editing articles for **Sunset** magazine, the building editor brought eight hats to work one day. Why? "We used to have some fairly deadly department meetings until the editor had us each put one on and conduct ourselves with a little more levity than usual," says Jensen. "We had a good laugh and got a lot done."

It doesn't matter if you're a top executive or a cashier at **Trader Joe's** markets, you'll still wear the same uniform. Since the 1960s, all employees, or crewmembers, wear a Hawaiian aloha shirt and a name tag.

7 Ways to Improve Working Conditions

1. Core value: Fun or humor
2. Recurring "shoes optional" day of the week
3. Special "theme" days
4. Casual dress on Wednesdays
5. Worker family/parent day visits to campus
6. Flex time and time off/ birthdays off with pay
7. Work hours cut during summer

"Tax season is a time of stress, long days, and longer weeks. In fact, we work pretty much every Saturday from January through April 15th," said an associate with **Horovitz, Rudoy & Rogan**, a Pittsburgh, Pennsylvania, CPA firm. To lighten things up, they observe Saturday Fun Days with themes like Alternate Profession Day, College Day, Pajama Day, and Cartoon Day. People dress in clothing and decorate their offices to match the day's theme. "At noon we vote on the best outfit and office. We keep a leaderboard in the lunchroom and at the end of the season, the top three scores win gift cards," the associate added. "Even our customers get involved calling to see what Saturday's theme is going to be so they can come dressed to 'fit in.'"

At the Denver, Colorado, and San Francisco, California, offices of **Gusto**, a payroll software business, workers enjoy a "no shoes" policy. Cofounders Josh Reeves, Edward Kim, and Tomer London were all raised in "no shoes" households, so when they started working together out of a house, there was never a shoe in sight. When the company moved to its first conventional office, the no-shoes tradition came too. "Companies can be sterile and cold," Josh told the *New York Times*. "We want our workplace to be really comfortable. In some ways, people feel more like themselves when their shoes are off." Visitors to the company can see over 600 pairs of shoes stored in slots at the entrance, and they are asked to remove their own shoes. Then they're given a choice of wearing slippers, spa sandals, or company-branded socks. Gusto's mission is to help people find a community at work and let work empower them to lead better lives, and the "no shoes" tradition ties into it.

Traditional work footwear is not a requirement at **Houzz**, an interior design application firm located in Palo Alto, California. On their first day of work, workers receive complimentary slippers to wear around the office.

Online retailer **Zappos**, headquartered in Las Vegas, Nevada, has a huge reputation as a fun place to work. The dress code is extremely casual, and anyone entering the building wearing a tie has it cut in half and pinned to the wall in the lobby. Desks have stuffed animals, and Blue Man Group–designed sculptures line the walls and emit sounds. "Create fun and a little weirdness" is written in the Zappos corporate charter.

When **Hilton Hotels** CEO Chris Nassetta tried on a staff uniform at a new downtown property, he was shocked. "I put on a housekeeper's jacket and I'm like, Wow, this is heavy," he says. "It didn't feel very comfortable or flexible, and I'm thinking, 'We got this wrong—we're not giving them the right clothing to wear.'" The company launched a partnership with Under Armour to redesign lighter, more comfortable work wear. Nassetta also started a program to upgrade "back-of-house" staff areas to make them as nice as the guest areas. The changes included more comfortable furnishings, better lighting, massage chairs, and free food in the updated cafeteria. Hilton also helped people to earn GEDs and formed Hilton University. These are a few of several employee-focused changes that have helped the chain be recognized as *Fortune*'s "Best Company to Work For" in America. According to the Great Place to Work Institute, Hilton outperforms when it comes to satisfaction among typically more disenfranchised "line-level" workers, such as cleaning and kitchen staff. Says Nassetta, "I am obsessed with taking care of them."

"When you're following your energy and doing what you want all the time, the distinction between work and play dissolves."

—SHAKTI GAWAIN

The president of **Belmont University** in Nashville, Tennessee, took a sabbatical to learn more about high-performing organizations by visiting successful companies. He learned that there was a strong correlation between performance and having fun, so when he returned, he created a Fun Committee and placed them in charge of creating more fun on the campus from events, activities, celebrations, and more.

Perkins Coie, a law firm headquartered in Seattle, Washington, has a Happiness Committee made up of anonymous employees, any one of whom can decide, "It's time to do something." Committee members perform anonymous acts of kindness, such as leaving gifts at workstations. Offices also hold monthly birthday parties, regular happy hours, and spontaneous celebrations throughout the year, like a picnic on the roof and Popsicle socials. An elaborate, annual holiday party features skits from new attorneys and appearances by the firm's managing partner, who has appeared as many characters, including a Vegas showgirl, Dolly Parton, and an Oompa Loompa.

About once a month, employees at **TechniGraphics**, the engineering data company headquartered in Wooster, Ohio, completely empty the building during lunch time. They may go bowling, ice skate, or meet at Acres of Fun, where they can drive go-carts or play mini-golf. Richard Danby, human resources director, says these and other social events are needed because employees work in units separated from each other. "This is an opportunity for a morale builder and an opportunity for employees to get to know each other better," he says. Sometimes they host on-site events like chili cook-offs and Ping-Pong tournaments, as long as they promote fun.

"At **Zoom**, employee appreciation and happiness is not a day, it's a way of life," says Heather Swan, chief happiness officer/strategic alliances. A video communications business headquartered in San Jose, California, the company offers the expected Silicon Valley benefits. "Our executive team and volunteer employee Happiness Crew also deliver happiness to our employees, customers, and community through unique activities, perks, experiences, and more," Swan adds. Specific programs include:

- Reimbursing workers for any book they/their family members buy, with no cap

- Reimbursing workers for fitness or gym memberships/classes, with no cap

- Executives taking turns hosting monthly breakfasts for their teams

> **5 Fun Organizational Techniques**
>
> 1. Embed Fun into your core company values.
>
> 2. Follow the Fun at Work principle.
>
> 3. Charter a Fun Committee to create and implement ideas.
>
> 4. Give *Work Made Fun Gets Done!* books to the committee.
>
> 5. Find ways to allocate budget resources for fun processes and events.

"The concept of Employee Appreciation Day is contrary to how we treat and engage with our employees," says Swan. "We do everything we can to show our appreciation for them every single day."

5 More Fun Organizational Techniques

1. Conduct a survey on fun at work and how it could be improved.

2. Include fun items on managers' 360s.

3. Orient all leaders to fun principles and tips.

4. Have leaders use humor at organization events.

5. When recruiting leaders, hire fun-friendly ones.

John Petrusa, founder, **People Business Solutions Inc**. in Wheaton, Illinois, and acting director of people & culture, shared the example of a contract manufacturing client, **Prismier**, based in Bolingbrook, Illinois, with 40+ employees. John worked with this client to create a more fun work environment. "We created a Culture Club team and charged them with creating company-wide events every month to engage employees in friendly competition, fellowship, and fun," he explained.

"The events have included things like Escape Room Teams, Cookie Walk, Salsa Making, and Steps Competitions, Parking Lot Carnival, Ethnic Food Day, Halloween Costume competition, Feed My Starving Children teams, attending Major League Baseball games, NCAA Tournament competition, and Super Bowl squares for friendly competition.

"We also implemented a Friday Night After Work Roundtable Group. A group of 4 or 6 employees would gather periodically and sample a variety of adult beverages and have a free-flowing discussion on any topic, not necessarily work-related."

Defense contractor and cybersecurity company **Raytheon**, in Waltham, Massachusetts, recognized its people were becoming increasingly concerned with work-life balance. To help ease the burden, they started a flexible working schedule with many options, including a "modified work week." Employees can work the days and hours that best fit their schedules, as long as they work 80 hours each biweekly pay period.

Vacation days and work hours aren't tracked at **Netflix**'s California headquarters. The company only tracks worker achievements. Every employee, no matter their level, is encouraged to take time off to refresh, including new parents, who often take four to eight months. In addition to the usual benefits of health insurance and travel reimbursement, **Automattic**, a global distributing company based in San Francisco, California, lets workers have open vacation time, with no set number of days per year for holidays. Working at Automattic also earns people the right to set their own working hours. Though the company is based in San Francisco, many employees work out of their own homes or offices in California, Bulgaria, and Japan. There is no vacation policy across the bay at **Ask.com**, the question-answering company in Oakland, California. Vacation time is not accrued or tracked. The company believes the best measure of success is what employees accomplish. They also offer tuition reimbursement, match charitable donations, and give workers a free weekly breakfast. The company is proud to share that they have an official ambassador of fun.

"I have looked in the mirror every morning and asked, 'If today was the last day of my life, would I want to do what I am about to do today?' Whenever the answer's been 'No' for too many days in a row, I know I need to change something."
—STEVE JOBS

At Boston-based marketing and public relations firm **Metis Communications**, workers get three weeks of vacation time and their birthdays off plus a bonus vacation between Christmas and New Year's.

CASE STUDY

CISCO'S "PEOPLE DEAL"
DEMONSTRATES ITS COMMITMENT TO WORKERS

Cisco Systems, the multinational technology conglomerate headquartered in San Jose, California, has seen an increase in company performance and employee satisfaction due in big part to its People Deal, a key component of its desired work culture. After years of revenue stagnation, the company has bounced back—under the leadership of CEO Chuck Robbins—due to growth in infrastructure, software, security, and services. A significant factor in its turnaround is the ongoing effort to make a positive impact on people, society, and the planet, highlighted by its People Deal—the promise the company makes to workers and what Cisco asks for in return.

What Is the People Deal?

There are three parts:

1. **First, Connect Everything**—Cisco commits to connecting people with personnel, information, and opportunities, while it asks its employees to connect with their peers to deliver positive outcomes that align with the company's goals and customer needs. Cisco promises to give workers the resources, tools, and direction to make that happen.

2. **Second, Innovate Everywhere**—Cisco commits to providing an "open and agile" environment that encourages employees to explore ideas and challenge norms, while asking employees to "relentlessly pursue" innovation to create a better future. Cisco promises to give workers permission to experiment and fail, even celebrating failures.

3. **Third, Benefit Everyone**—Cisco commits to support employee development, appreciate individuals' contributions, and positively impact the world with the company's collective ability. In turn, Cisco expects workers to embody the company's global values and believe in its collective ability to "win together." Cisco promises to support teaming and reward employees for behaving in a way that reflects Cisco's value.

How It Started

In 2014, Cisco workers were surveyed and asked to define the milestones of their own respective experience. After leadership considered the results, resources were dedicated to each of the 11 "key moments" identified from employee input. Establishing clear expectations and shared accountability (partnership) between the company and its workers were critical to the effort's success.

How Employees Use It

The People Deal and its terminology are shared with coveted candidates during the recruiting process. As people are onboarded and develop in their jobs, the terminology is continuously used on a daily basis, especially during weekly manager–associate check-ins. Instead of waiting for an annual review—Cisco doesn't have them—workers and managers share updates and feedback immediately and can course-correct much sooner. The company reports seeing improvements in culture surveys that it attributes, in great part, to the execution of the People Deal.

Sykes, the multichannel demand generation and customer-engagement services company based in Tampa, Florida, helps its cross-continental and across-ocean traveling employees feel more comfortable. For 7-to-10-day trips, the company lets workers arrive one day earlier than normal, to recover from the flight or to tour the city they're visiting. "We know when you're gone that long from home, from your family, having some downtime will relieve some of the homesickness and prepare you for the work ahead," says Al Mazzola, director of global finance and travel services.

> "May you find the balance of life—time for work but also time for play. Too much of one thing ends up creating stress that no one needs in their life."
>
> —CATHERINE PULSIFER

Patagonia, the adventure outfitter headquartered in Ventura, California, offers flextime based on weather conditions. Employees can go surfing when the waves are good and skiing when there's fresh powder. To help facilitate the likelihood of workers participating in these activities, the company provides on-site childcare.

Inspired by the likes of Uber and Lyft, the on-demand economy is now essential to most consumers. Workplace amenities like massages, haircuts, and car washes are available to workers on demand in most major cities. At **SnackNation**, the snack-delivery service based in Culver City, California, workers have access to an on-demand, high-quality car wash service at a very reasonable price. At their New York City location, the company discovered its offices were too far from the nearest subway stop, making trips to the office an unpleasant walk during the winter. It hired a shuttle bus service to transport employees from the subway and back. Now, during blizzard conditions, they post office closures and adjust pickup times. **HubSpot**, the developer and marketer headquartered in Cambridge, Massachusetts, focuses on the best fit for both talent and clients. Employees at all levels and functions enjoy unique perks like the Free Book Program, unlimited free meals with contacts, and HubTalks from experts.

According to the *Financial Times*, one Valentine's Day, a couple met on their Beijing, China–based company's singles chat room and soon after got married. The bride, Tian Huimin, who headed the singles' club, had asked for a ride home on the chat room, and it was her future husband who offered to take her. Huimin told the *FT* that she welcomes what might seem like an intrusion of work into private time in the West because, in Beijing, singles are often far from home and lonely on weekends.

Business travel can be very tough on breastfeeding mothers, so **Johnson & Johnson** started a service that let mothers ship breast milk home for free.

One of **Airbnb**'s strategies is to get people not only out of the office but out of the city. This San Francisco, California–based vacation housing provider gives each worker $2,000 a year to travel anywhere in the world. Besides the travel stipend, employees can bring their pets to work every day, go sailing, play Ping-Pong, take a weekly yoga class at work, *and* enjoy daily organic lunches. And where most of the business world observes Casual Fridays, Airbnbers do the opposite, dressing up on Formal Fridays.

Adobe, the San Jose, California–based computer software company, encourages workers to participate in their award-winning Kickbox program, where employees can submit innovative ideas. Employees get a red cardboard box filled with stationary, snacks, and a $1,000 prepaid credit card to explore one of their ideas, no questions asked.

> "Culture eats strategy for lunch."
>
> —PETER DRUCKER

A few weeks before April 1st one year, **Genentech**, the pharmaceuticals pioneer headquartered in San Francisco, California, posted a story on its intranet announcing that goats would be used for campus landscaping. The company asked employees to sign up to adopt a goat, stating research that showed "the animals are more productive grazers when they interact with a human." The company arranged for real goats to be on-site, and several hundred employees signed up. People loved it. "It's *great* working for a company that would bring in *real* goats for an April Fool's joke," one employee said. "Nice job Genentech. I love this place!"

> "A good time to laugh is any time you can."
>
> —DR. MADAN KATARIA

During the COVID-19 outbreak, **Kroger** food markets based in Cincinnati, Ohio, gave a one-time bonus of $300 to full-time and $150 to part-time employees. "Grocery workers are on the frontlines, ensuring Americans have access to the food and products they need during this unprecedented pandemic," said Rodney McMullen, Kroger's chairman and CEO. "They work around the clock to keep our stores open for our customers. I am incredibly grateful for all they are doing. The true heroes in this story are our associates, and we want to provide them with additional resources and support to help them continue their remarkable effort."

CHAPTER 10

Office Space & Design

The room is there for the human being—
not the human being for the room.

—EL LISSITZKY

For today's employees, the design of the office can and does play a key role in their satisfaction with their job and the company. A report by CMI Workplace found that strong office design can make employees up to 33 percent happier at work, and a recent U.S. Workplace Survey by Gensler found that workplace design was one of the key drivers of innovation within an organization.

Innovative companies are five times more likely to have workplaces that prioritize individual and group workspace. That same survey found that the most innovative companies had workplaces designed for the individual worker that also provided resources for collaborative group work. Employees at these companies reported better relationships with management and said they found more meaning in their work.

In addition, a World Green Building Council study found 69 percent of businesses that implemented healthy building features reported improvements in both employee satisfaction and engagement. Environmental factors like indoor air quality, lighting, acoustics, interior layout, and biophilia (adding plants in and out of the workspace) are all associated with improved worker satisfaction and performance. Making sure your workers have access to natural daylight can improve their sleep, which can lead to better moods and higher productivity.

A study by Hassell Architects and Empirica Research looked at how workplace space planning and office design affects how attractive the company is to job seekers. In a nutshell, they found that it does. Of course, today's employees consider salary important, but if the offered salary is competitive, they look to other factors, including workplace facilities and aesthetics, the technology provided, and workplace culture to determine where they would be happier.

The same study found that 37 percent of job candidates will accept a job with a lower salary if the company has an appealing culture, excellent workplace facilities, and up-to-date technology. In addition:

- Researchers at the Birmingham Business School found that people are 12 percent more likely to report being happy with their job when they have freedom and autonomy in their work environment, that is, the ability to move around within the office.

- An overwhelming majority (87 percent) of workers would like their current employer to offer healthier workspace benefits, with options ranging from wellness rooms, company fitness benefits, sit-stands, healthy lunch options, and ergonomic seating, according to the Fellowes Workplace Wellness Trend Report. And, in the same report, 93 percent of workers in the tech industry said they would stay longer at a company that offered those things.

- A study conducted by the Department of Design + Environmental Analysis at Cornell showed that employees seated within 10 feet of a window reported an 84 percent decrease in eyestrain, headaches, and blurred vision symptoms.

- The Global Impact of Biophilic Design in the Workplace study showed that people who worked in spaces with natural features reported 15 percent higher levels of overall well-being. Furthermore, the respondents expressed feeling 6 percent more productive and 15 percent more creative at work.

- If the interior design of an office appeals to its occupants and creates both breakout space and social space, there are improvements in employee concentration, collaboration, confidentiality, creativity—all leading to a more enjoyable, fun workplace.

Let's look at examples of how the design of an office workspace makes an impact on the fun and enjoyment of its employees.

"'Desk' plus 'interior' equals 'Deskterior,' a movement to make office spaces feel like home in a country— Korea—with the longest working hours of any nation," says the BBC's Julie Yoonnyung Lee. Spending that much time at a desk can be quite tedious. Rha Hye-young, a 30-year-old sales manager in Seoul, decorates her desk with action figures from Hollywood movies. "Whenever I get new action figures, I bring them to my office instead of displaying at home because I spend much of my time at work." Banker Lee Ju-hee treasures her small, fairytale-like desk. It's covered in pink products including a mini humidifier, a mini fan, a small air purifier, and a tumbler sterilizer. She even has a pink keyboard.

> "An open office is a great format for a changeable work environment, where employees have a say over how they work and a place that can adapt to their needs and to the needs of the business."
>
> **—NEIL BLUMENTHAL**

Employees creatively decorate their work cubicles at Las Vegas, Nevada–based **Zappos**, the online retailer. Just about anything goes—posters, clothing, stuffed animals, wigs, you name it. The only limits are the employees' own imaginations.

MeetEdgar, a social media scheduling platform from Austin, Texas, has been a completely remote company since its first day in business. The company gives full-time remote workers up to $100 a month toward internet access, $300 a month for coworking space, and new MacBooks that become property of the employee after six months. Perhaps the most unique offering for the home office is paying for housecleaning services—the entire house, not just the remote workspace.

Pocket Gems, a San Francisco–based mobile game publishing business, gets everyone involved in making a great work environment. It gives each employee $100 to creatively design and outfit their working space. Employees frequently pool their funds for bigger-ticket items such as a Ping-Pong table. Edinburgh, United Kingdom–based **Good-Loop**, a platform that lets viewers of video advertisements send donations to their chosen charities, gives each of its employees £50 to brighten their home offices. Company cofounder Amy Williams says, "Having those small little items or objects that make it more symbolically professional can be psychologically helpful. Be it a desktop screen you plug your laptop into, a potted plant you put on your desk, or just something that makes you feel like you created a space that helps you delineate work from home."

> "Enjoyment of life generally includes being socially connected, having fun, and feeling a sense of purpose."
>
> —MALLIKA CHOPRA

> "All great architecture is the design of space that contains, cuddles, exalts, or stimulates the persons in that space."
>
> —PHILIP JOHNSON

Harmless Harvest, a coconut water company, installed hammocks at its San Francisco, California, headquarters.

To encourage employees to meet each other, **Google** has long tables in its lunch areas. They also provide ample "diner booths" because they have found they work better than conference rooms for promoting creativity.

CASE STUDY

CHECK OUT HULU'S
HULUBRATORY

When Hulu's design team began work on its new headquarters in Los Angeles, it had a few major things to consider. "We're all about embracing fun. The facility needed to reflect that," Jim O'Gorman, Hulu's SVP of talent and organization, said to Business Insider. "This is a meritocracy—everyone has the same desk and the same chair." Architecture firm Gensler worked with Hulu to design its new 90,000-square-foot home in Santa Monica, California. Workers voted on almost all parts of the design, from the style of chairs to the types of food in the kitchen.

The Hulu team likes puns. The entrance to the "Hulubratory" gets your attention as soon as you get off the elevator. The waiting area is covered with hundreds of portraits of Hulu employees (Hulugans). During onboarding, each Hulugan takes a fun but professional picture, using any prop that shows their personality. CEO Mike Hopkins embraced the fun atmosphere of the workplace when he joined the team in October 2013. In his Hulu portrait, he posed throwing his suit in the trash.

Fun and entertainment were important considerations in the office design. The design team created four different game hubs, each with a unique personality. All of the game rooms are soundproofed using studio glazing and double walls. "We really encourage people to play," said Lauren Nuttall, Hulu's facilities, operations, and programs manager. "Work should be fun. Being here should be fun."

TIME TO TAKE A BREAK

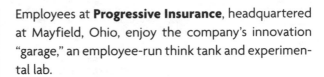

2 Low/No-Cost Ways to Have Art at Work

1. Ask local gallery owners to provide paintings, sculptures, professional photography, etc.

2. Invite artists, art students, and employees to display their works on a rotating basis in the hallways at your place of work.

Employees at **Progressive Insurance**, headquartered at Mayfield, Ohio, enjoy the company's innovation "garage," an employee-run think tank and experimental lab.

LEGO, a Billund, Denmark–headquartered plastic brick toy company, has an open-office design with team boundaries defined by bold banners and large LEGO brick sculptures. Designers are encouraged to express their individuality by displaying all sorts of objects and images in their workspaces.

Evolution Hospitality, a hotel management company in San Clemente, California, designed a company kitchen called the Break Room. It opens onto a living room with a Ping-Pong table and three TVs tuned to TheSurfNetwork.

The office of **Promocodes.com**, a coupon codes and deals website headquartered in Santa Monica, California, is a couple of blocks from the beach, and its office décor reflects that. Featuring wood floors and ceiling panels, beach-themed artwork, and a metal staircase, the company has a tiki bar and a large rooftop for frequent BBQs. **Twitter** holds rooftop meetings.

Visual offerings and artwork on the nine-floor office at **Twitch**, the gaming company based in San Francisco, California, were conceptualized and executed by select Twitch gamers and streamers. There are two "Instagram-ready" rooms with high-end lighting and a Twitch streaming setup for employees to play with. Downstairs are a few 6v6 gaming rooms with stadium seating near a cafe with free coffee and smoothies. On the other side of the barista bar is a salon with arcade games, pinball, cornhole, and several classic video game consoles. Happy hours are very busy. "I think we have every console going back to . . . there's an Atari here," says university programs manager Thomas Tessier, adding that the room's "'Game of Thrones' pinball is [also] very popular as of late." For non-gamers, conference rooms are themed for Millennial and Gen-X interests, such as Netflix's *Stranger Things*, the *Harry Potter* series, and Bob Ross, who was the subject of a marathon streamed on Twitch several years back. "There's actually a Bob Ross wig they have on a mannequin in there," Tessier adds.

CEO Joe Reynolds of **Red Frog Events** installed a tree house with a zip line at his offices in Chicago, Illinois.

As summertime approaches, Needham, Massachusetts–based **TripAdvisor**, the travel information company, transforms its outdoor patio to include a fire pit and lounge seating next to its pub.

Etsy, the e-commerce of handmade goods company based in New York, boasts that all 200,000 square feet of its Dumbo headquarters is quirky and fun. They offer a variety of meeting space styles—in and out of doors—and fully stocked workshops used for regular "crafternoons."

L.L. Bean, the outdoor apparel company headquartered in Freeport, Maine, partnered with Industrious to offer the first outdoor coworking spaces in urban parks in the U.S. Some have roofs. They developed a

---

5 Things in a Fun Office Space

1. Pez containers, Mr. Potato Head, Barrel of Monkeys, bobble heads
2. Plants with fun names and personalities
3. Decorated-cubicle contests
4. Mini-golf course made of office furniture and supplies
5. Humor bulletin board in break room/back office area

"Of all the arts, architecture is the one which acts the most slowly, but the most surely, on the soul."

—ERNEST DIMNET

5 More Things in a Fun Office Space

1. Break room wall painted with chalkboard paint
2. Wall of fame
3. Pool table for 9-ball games
4. Mini-golf course (real one)
5. Break room with games, art supplies, videos, mags, and comfy couches

handbook explaining the science behind the venture, along with a how-to. As Kathryn Pratt, director of brand engagement at L.L. Bean, was quoted in a *Slate* article, the goal is to encourage people to "integrate the outdoors into their workday, not just reserve it for after work or on the weekends." She added, "Many different types of meetings can benefit from being in the outdoors, whether that's creative brainstorming sessions or interviews."

Instead of going to hotels for off-site meetings, companies are looking for a more intimate team experience at Airbnb properties. **Box Inc.**, the cloud management and file sharing service, and **Meritor**, a global supplier of commercial vehicle products, find that they can stay in the same place at less cost, and they don't need to arrange separate meeting rooms and conference centers.

CHAPTER 11

Food

Good food equals good mood.

—ANONYMOUS

ike many things in the work environment, why should employers need to worry about the food their employees eat? In a nutshell (pun intended), you don't have to worry about this, but if you choose to consider the topic, the return on productivity, wellness, and employee satisfaction can be significant.

According to the CDC, loss of productivity due to chronic diseases costs businesses $260 billion annually. Rival Health reports that 69 percent of employees are interested in nutrition programs, but only 43 percent of employers offer them. And the *Health Affairs* journal reports the average ROI of a comprehensive corporate wellness program is $3.30 for every dollar spent.

When it comes to employee happiness, 67 percent of full-time employees with access to free food at work are "extremely" or "very" happy at their current job, according to SnackNation, a snack delivery service for offices or homes, so it shouldn't come as a surprise that free food is one of the top perks that employees desire. It's one of the major reasons why companies like Google and Facebook use it as a way to attract and keep top talent. Furthermore, that same study found that 48 percent of job seekers weigh company perks, including the availability of snacks, in their decision to work for a company.

A survey of more than 1,000 full-time workers conducted by Peapod, an online grocer, found that more than half of people (56 percent) are "extremely happy" or "very happy" at their current jobs. However, that number jumps to 67 percent for employees who have free food at work.

Shareable meals are a source of workplace camaraderie, especially since the majority of workers spend nearly half their day using technology to communicate. Creating an environment where employees can interact while eating has a positive impact on company culture: 35 percent of companies provide office meals to encourage team building, a survey from ZeroCater found.

If it's not in your budget to provide free food at work every day, consider once a week—for example, "bagel and coffee Fridays." With only one-third of offices giving employees free snacks and drinks, even a simple offering can help you stand out from the competition.

Let's look at what some companies are doing to use food to make their work environment more fun and fulfilling for their employees.

Norcross, Georgia–based **Canon Solutions America** sends snack carts with sodas and water around to all of its workstations. When workers dance the hula, they give them snacks and small gifts.

> "Hard work should be rewarded by good food."
> —KEN FOLLETT

For any employee working outside in the cold at **Wegman's Food Markets**, the family-owned supermarket chain headquartered in Rochester, New York, free hot chocolate is available.

Trial Runners, a Dickinson, North Dakota, ophthalmology clinical research organization, gives its workers warm cookies on rainy days and boasts decadent company potlucks.

United Kingdom employees of Surrey-based **Enterprise Holdings** got the chance to sample sodas from the U.S. that most had never tasted. They held a fun taste test to see if root beer was better than cream soda (cream soda won).

Paul Conningham, from **SBC Global**, brings Crock-Pots full of meatballs to work to make sandwiches for everyone. "It's better than buying lunch because anyone can buy pizza but a manager who cares enough to take the time to *make* lunch or just bring in a pile of fresh baked cookies will be much more appreciated," says Conningham. "Plus it gives some valuable one-on-one, no-pressure interaction with folks while enjoying a meatball sub or a few cookies."

At big-box retailer **Costco**, headquartered in Issaquah, Washington, employees get free turkeys for Thanksgiving.

Three times a year, groups of 8 to 10 employees from **HubSpot**, a developer and marketer with headquarters in Cambridge, Massachusetts, sign up for a Mystery Dinner. Workers have no idea what restaurant or what group of people will be attending until 4 p.m. the day of the event. "What we've found is that an evening of spending quality time over a nice meal goes a long way toward our employees building meaningful connections with people on other teams," says Katie Burke, the company vice president of culture.

Food played an important role at the 11-Day Office Olympics hosted by Glen Falls, New York–based

10 Ways to Have Fun with Food at Work

1. Share/publish favorite recipes.
2. Arrange potlucks featuring different cuisines.
3. Make/order breakfast and/or lunch.
4. Make/order special dinners.
5. Host on-site/go to farmers' markets.
6. Host on-site/go to food trucks.
7. Volunteer at soup kitchens.
8. Arrange for meal-preparing team-building events.
9. Organize food drives.
10. Survey workers for new food items.

Mannix Marketing, a digital marketing company. It started with pizza at the opening ceremony. Day 3 featured the Kitchen Challenge. Players ate a jar of baby food that contained chicken, rice, peas, and carrots. After the jar was finished, the athletes ate a small stack of saltine crackers. The first person to whistle after eating the crackers won. At the closing ceremony, everyone enjoyed the different variations of chili, including vegetarian, spicy, and venison.

Employees at **Trader Joe's** markets need to know what the food they sell tastes like in order to recommend it to customers. So, taste testing is part of their job.

When the CEO at **Twice**, the online secondhand clothes company based in San Francisco, California, says, "Surprise! The truck's here. Have some ice cream on us," employees are in for more than the expected ice-cream-truck fare. They get ice cream tacos and handcrafted organic soft serve.

The project management team at **DR Systems**, a medical imaging solutions company (now owned by IBM) located in San Diego, California, frequently asks its manufacturing department to rush or change delivery schedules when customers make changes. This disruption in schedules causes frustration and frequently necessitates extra work from the manufacturing team. To alleviate the stress, keep lines of communication open, and show appreciation to the manufacturing team for going above and beyond, the project management team treats the manufacturing team to doughnuts for breakfast, or they will host a pizza lunch for the two departments.

> "Never work before breakfast. If you have to work before breakfast, eat your breakfast first."
>
> —JOSH BILLINGS

> *"Friday* is my second favorite 'f-word.' My first is *food."*
>
> —ANONYMOUS

Interos, a tech start-up in Arlington, Virginia, clearly believes one way to employees' hearts is through their stomachs. A staffer celebrating an anniversary or birthday gets a delivery of cupcakes, along with a gift card. And the company's Culture Club sent each of the 65 staffers a SnackNation box filled with nutrition bars, nuts, and healthy chips and cookies.

> "A balanced diet is a cookie in each hand."
>
> **—ANONYMOUS**

SPOTLIGHT ON FARMERS' MARKETS

With the movement toward health and wellness at the workplace comes the natural inclusion of farmers' markets. Yahoo, AOL, Adobe, Progressive Insurance, and Nicklaus Children's Hospital are just a few of the companies that regularly offer these markets on-site. "When I speak at our new-hire orientations and I present our wellness options, mentioning the farmers' market piques everyone's interest. It definitely is a selling point," says Katie Stoner, the hospital's exercise physiologist for employee wellness.

Kaiser Permanente, a healthcare provider that operates more than 50 farmers' markets at its hospitals and clinics across the U.S., surveyed over 2,400 patrons who visited its markets in a given year. Greater than 80 percent said they were eating "a lot more" or "a little more" fruits and vegetables in their regular diets.

Instead of setting up full markets, some worksites offer community supported agriculture (CSA) programs, where boxes of seasonal produce from local farms are delivered to the workplaces weekly. The FairShare CSA Coalition in Madison, Wisconsin, works with 50 member farms and has brought CSA programs to 45 businesses in the metro area. Its business partners include **Duluth Trading Co.** and **Aprilaire**.

Biotech giant Genentech, headquartered in South San Francisco, California, hosts on-site farmers' markets featuring fresh, organic, locally grown produce at peak freshness. The markets are part of the company's overall commitment to its workers' wellness.

Food trucks are a shared love at LA-based **EdgeCast**, a content delivery network. Different food providers swing by monthly and offer delicious catered lunches, from tacos to In-N-Out burgers to grilled cheese sandwiches.

"Food makes me happy. Make me work round the clock, but feed me first!"

—DEEPIKA PADUKONE

The staff restaurant at the **Hyatt Hotel** Mumbai, India, is the regular venue for employee culinary celebrations. These themed food festivals are organized with a specifically curated menu, ambience, music, and fun seating arrangements.

Kickstarter, a public benefit corporation based in Brooklyn, New York, offers catered family meals and happy hours. Once a month the company randomly invites groups of four to six employees and treats them to a long, restful lunch where they can further develop relationships with each other.

"In Italy, they add work and life on to good food and wine."

—ROBIN LEACH

Sabrina, from employee engagement software firm **TINYpulse**, says, "One thing that we do on our own marketing team is Monday morning coffee." Her team walks to various coffee shops around their Seattle, Washington, neighborhood. "We just relax for about half an hour. Sometimes we talk about work, sometimes we talk about our weekends—our goal is to start off the week on a positive note so we can feel productive for the rest of the day and week," she adds. Similarly at **Square**, the San Francisco, California–based financial service company, executive team members have casual one-on-ones with new employees at local coffee shops.

Every Friday, employees of **Vimly Benefits Solutions**, the information systems consulting company headquartered in Mukilteo, Washington, are treated to breakfast made and served by coworkers. "The company gives us so much and this is just extra," says employee Yelena Semenuk. "It's really sweet."

Another employer keeping its workers fed is the **Midtown Group**, a staffing and recruitment firm in Washington, D.C. Each Friday, Midtown's president and CEO, Helen Stefan-Moreau, has full meals delivered to each of her 30 employees. The dinners come from other local businesses, including Ridgewells Catering and Fat Pete's Barbecue.

Executives at Brantford, Ontario–based **Williamson Group**, a financial services company, host weekly Fibre Fridays. Employees are treated to huge trays of fruits and vegetables.

It's not the costliest benefit, but if workers are going to be flipping burgers, they can't do better than **In-N-Out**'s free Double-Double burger and fries offered to employees every shift. In-N-Out is a fast-food restaurant chain with its headquarters located in Irvine, California.

How delightful it is when you've been working hard all day to learn that leftover food from a meeting has been put out for general consumption in the kitchen. **Zappos**, in Las Vegas, Nevada, has a software application for its employees that identifies when and where free food is available throughout their campus.

6 More Ways to Have Fun with Food at Work

1. On way to work, buy team coffee/beverages.
2. Arrange for Ice-cream/shave-ice trucks to visit office.
3. Bring food from home.
4. Have monthly breakfast meetings (different restaurants each time).
5. Have a best cookie contest.
6. Have a chili cook-off.

Ben & Jerry's Ice Cream, based in South Burlington, Vermont, wants employees to know and love its ice cream, so it rewards them with three pints every day. While it may seem like the opposite of many workplaces' health initiatives, it does make employees popular with their friends and families, with whom they are encouraged to share this daily perk. Employees can also recommend the names of new ice cream flavors.

Twitch, a San Francisco, California–based gaming company, offers free food all day long. Two popular food-related events are Donut Days and Beignet Cook-Off competitions. Tickets are sold and proceeds go to local charities.

"First we eat, then we do everything else."

—ANONYMOUS

StumbleUpon, a discovery and advertisement engine company headquartered in San Francisco, California, gives "Stumblers" (employees) five days of breakfast and lunch and provides a kitchen stocked with organic fruit, snacks, and beverages.

Zynga, a game developer based in San Francisco, California, offers free meals and snacks—including daily lunch and dinner.

CHAPTER 12

Dogs & Pets

If there are no dogs in Heaven, then
when I die I want to go where they went.

—**WILL ROGERS**

Another fun practice that most companies can support is allowing employees to bring their pets—especially dogs—to work! More and more frequently, employers and employees are discovering that pets at the workplace make them happier, lower stress levels, and create a comfortable, flexible environment. Pets can create camaraderie within the workplace and trigger interactions that may not have happened without them.

University of Southern California's Dana and David Dornsife College of Letters, Arts and Sciences reports have shown that pets have calming effects on employees—reducing blood pressure, lowering stress, and making employees more cordial and productive.

American Pet Products Association (APPA) National Pet Owners Survey found that petting a dog has been proven to reduce stress, whether or not you own the dog. According to the *Telegraph* (UK), the process of patting and stroking a dog reduces your blood pressure, changes your physiological state into a more relaxed mode, and makes you feel better. So, dogs in your office could help lessen the overall stress of the workplace environment.

A study by the Virginia Commonwealth University found that when people had their pets around during the workday, they had much lower stress levels compared with employees who did not. The study showed that employees who brought their pets to the workplace experienced an 11 percent drop in stress levels, while those who were forced to leave their pets at home had a 70 percent rise in stress levels.

The researchers found the benefits may extend to coworkers as well, who reported enjoying brief interactions with the pets and sometimes even asked to take them for a walk. Dogs in the workplace also provide more social support for employees, as well as more opportunities for coworkers to interact in a positive setting, according to a number of studies.

The same APPA study showed dogs encourage owners to get exercise: on average, dog owners walk 79 percent farther than non–dog owners. Exercise has many add-on benefits for physical and mental health. Employees with their dogs at work are likely to get out and about at coffee breaks: the physical exercise will help with their state of mind and productivity for the rest of the day.

Pet ownership generally has been shown to have a number of positive health benefits, including fewer visits to the doctor, lower cholesterol, and improved heart health. If you encourage pet ownership among your employees by letting them bring their dogs to work, you're likely to be rewarded by a healthier workforce with fewer sick days.

A study by the Virginia Commonwealth University found that there's proof that animals help relieve stress in other ways as well. According to studies, employees in pet-friendly workplaces have proven to be happier, friendlier, more creative, and more cooperative than in non-pet offices. Central Michigan University found that employees at dog-friendly workplaces collaborated and trusted each other more. All of these things help create a more efficient, productive—and fun—culture.

The Human Animal Bond Research Institute has even studied the effect of dog presence on problem-solving by groups. Their research indicates improved cohesion, trust, and cooperation in groups with a dog. The institute has also conducted a nationwide survey that showed greater employee engagement and retention in pet-friendly workplaces.

A "dogs at work" policy is often viewed by employees as a valuable employment perk. According to the *Telegraph*, a recent study showed that over two-fifths (43 percent) of employees would like to see pets allowed in the office, 39 percent felt that pets at work would increase their productivity, 50 percent believed it would increase their happiness, and a significant proportion of workers would be prepared to stay at work for longer if pets were allowed to be there with them. For employers, dog-friendly policies can be added to the list of workplace benefits made to attract and maintain talent, particularly in respect to Millennials. Pet-friendly companies include Amazon, Google, Salesforce, Airbnb, Eventbrite, Yammer, Etsy, Asana, Zynga, and 72andSunny.

Let's take a look at some specific examples of how companies encourage and facilitate letting their employees have pets at work!

Camden Property Trust, headquartered in Houston, Texas, hosts a Bring Your Dog to Work Day. **Short-Stack**, a self-service social-media platform company based in Reno, Nevada, has an open-dog policy on Woof-Wednesdays. At **Spyder Trap**, a Minneapolis/St. Paul–based marketing firm, dogs roam free on Dog Fridays. And employees of **FlyHomes**, a real estate agency based in Seattle, dress up their dogs for their December holiday parties.

> "Outside of a dog, a book is a man's best friend. Inside of a dog, it's too dark to read."
>
> —GROUCHO MARX

In Bloomington, Minnesota, dogs "hang out" every day at **The Nerdery**, a technology company. The same holds true just across the northern border at

> "Everything I know I learned from cats."
>
> —NORA ROBERTS

Mars Canada in Bolton, Ontario, and at San Francisco, California–based **Zoosk**, an online data app. Of course, if you're in the dog business like **Rover**, a Seattle, Washington–based online connector of dog owners with sitters and walkers, having dogs in your workplace is a no-brainer. Besides playing with their own pets, workers schedule doggie playdates with other colleagues.

CASE STUDY

THROW AMAZON A BONE

On any given day at Amazon's Seattle, Washington–based headquarters, humans share their space with approximately 6,000 canine companions. The retail giant is part of the 8 percent of workplaces in the U.S. that allow dogs to join their humans in the office, according to the Society for Human Resource Management. That's a jump from 5 percent of employers just a few years earlier.

Rufus, a big campus favorite, had such an impact on people, the company named a building after him. The company maintains a doggie deck for pets on the 17th floor. It has a fake fire hydrant, water stations, and biowaste relief areas. Puppies play on rocks and other structures at the leash-free park.

"Dogs in the workplace are an unexpected mechanism for connection," says Lara Hirschfield, Amazon's "woof pack" manager. "I see Amazonians meeting each other in our lobbies or elevators every day because of their dogs."

On Halloween, workers and their dogs bond at Barktoberfest on the Van Vorst Plaza, hosted by Downtown Dog Lounge. Treats, drinks, and activities are included. Recently, dozens of dogs participated in the costume contest, which included Daenerys and her pet dragon, and a canine trio of Pooh Bear, Eeyore, and Piglet.

At **PetBox**, an online retailer of pet toys and products based in San Diego, California, "expect the unexpected," says Sean Conlon, cofounder and CEO. "At our office, for instance, we have a German Shepard who is a regular 'guest.' She is known for running laps around the office, like a Greyhound, and when she does, the team cheers her on." According to Conlon, this results in highly effective team bonding, which yields many dividends for the company.

BAM Communications, a media-relations firm based in San Diego, California, brought in adoptable rescue puppies for their workers, as well as a taco truck with free tacos. "I organized one of my surprises for the entire team," says CEO Beck Bamberger. "I kept the team inside the office and shut the blinds to all the windows while a dozen puppies were led onto our huge patio. Once the pups were in, I told the team to run out. We played with the puppies for about an hour—all were rescues, mostly from Mexico, and their caretakers were with us to tell us about the adoption process. We have a *lot* of dog lovers and owners here, so I'll probably make this a tradition."

If dogs are going to be at work all day, having hygiene accommodations is a must. The Bolton, Ontario, office of **Mars Canada**, a subsidiary of the U.S. chocolate maker, provides indoor facilities, an outdoor "doggie courtyard," and free treats. **Zynga**, a San Francisco, California, gaming company, has a rooftop doggie park, as does **Amazon**.

Factoids

The first ever Take Your Dog to Work Day in 1999 saw an estimated 300 businesses participate.

Willis Towers Watson says the number of companies offering pet insurance as an employee perk increased more than 134 percent between 2013 and 2017.

In 2017, *Forbes* reported that pet insurance was the hottest employee benefit offered by 5,000 U.S. companies.

At its San Diego, California, headquarters, **Petco**, a retail pet supply chain, encourages its workers to bring a variety of pets to work—not just dogs. Snakes, lizards, fish, you name it.

Tip

Host a "Bring Your Dog/Pet to Work Day."

Since many people today consider pets as part of their immediate family, they really value having company health benefits and company perks extended to them. And a few companies are starting to unleash those benefits. For example, when an employee gets a new pet, some companies are now offering "paw-turnity" and "furturnity" leaves so they can start off their adjustment to the new family member on the right paw.

7 Companies with Paid Time Off for Employees with New Puppies

1. BitSol Solutions
2. BrewDog
3. Kimpton Hotels & Restaurants
4. Mars Petcare
5. mParticle
6. Musti Group
7. Nina Hale

At **PetSmart**, a retail pet supply chain based in Phoenix, Arizona, workers get free training classes plus a 15 percent discount on pet-related merchandise, grooming, and veterinary services. And if they don't want to leave their dogs at home, many employees bring their pets to work with them. Workers at **Dogtopia**, a dog daycare provider also headquartered in Phoenix, enjoy a personal wellness fund that can be used for doggie daycare and veterinary visits. Employees who don't have pets can still use the fund for healthy lunches and gym memberships.

A nonprofit healthcare system based in San Diego, California, **Scripps Health**, offers pet insurance for its employees' dogs and cats.

Companies are recognizing the emotional impact of pet death and are now offering bereavement time to heal. Time off for the passing of a pet may not be as long as that for other close family members, but every bit helps. For example, **Kimpton Hotels & Restaurants** in San Francisco offers three days of leave; **Mars Inc**. offers one day and the option to work flexible hours thereafter; and **Trupanion**, a Seattle-based pet insurance company, offers employees one day off.

> "We offer maternity and paternity leave. A pet is just another member of the family. We don't discriminate just because they aren't human."
>
> **—LAUREL PEPPINO**

CHAPTER 13

The Arts

There's nothing like music to relieve the soul and uplift it.

—MICKEY HART

Integrating the arts into the workplace helps make work more enjoyable for most employees. A prime example is regarding music. A recent Spotify survey shows 61 percent of respondents listen to music at work to boost their productivity and happiness. Even more compelling: 90 percent of workers perform better and 88 percent produce more accurate work when using music as a productivity tool, which was found in a study by the University of Birmingham in England.

"Music seems to fulfill a range of important functions for employees, including providing relief from stress, and improving concentration," says music evaluation consultant and researcher Dr. Anneli Haake, who wrote a Ph.D. dissertation at the University of Sheffield, in England, on the effects of music listening in offices.

"The most common reasons for listening to music at work are to improve mood and relax. Music can also help employees to engage in work tasks, through blocking out distracting noise in the office," Dr. Haake said. She emphasizes that music choice and control play a large part in these benefits. "If music is forced upon people, the music can be irritating and annoying, and we know from research that office noise can have severe negative effects on employee health, well-being, and productivity," she reported.

Accountemps, a division of global staffing firm Robert Half, conducted a survey consisting of 1,000 workers in office environments, and the results are encouraging for music lovers. Of those allowed to listen to music while working, 85 percent of participants said they prefer to listen to tunes at work rather than listen to nothing. Further, 8 out of 10 total survey respondents said they enjoy it, and 71 percent said it makes them more productive. According to the survey, out of the 85 percent of people who like listening to music at work, three genres topped the list in terms of popularity: pop, rock, and country. Michael Steinitz, executive director of Accountemps, said this can be explained by generational preferences.

Following are other examples of how companies have embraced the arts in the workplace.

Laura Brady, director of human resources for **Marburn Academy** in New Albany, Ohio, shares: "As we transitioned back into the building after COVID-19 we had to implement a bunch of new protocols. One is white arrows that go one way. I for one have to do a complete loop around the building to go next door to my office to make a copy! Many are in similar situations but it's all in the interest of social distancing. I call it doing 'the loop.' So I started to create song lyrics about the process using songs we all know. I sing them as I go the full loop and now I have others doing it too, e.g., Blondie's 'One Way or Another': 'One way not the other, HR will get you they'll getcha getcha getcha go one way not the other.' I have done this to 'Follow the Yellow Brick Road,' 'Stayin' Alive,' 'White Rabbit,' etc. It is fun, light and makes people laugh. It also makes them more willing to do 'the loop.'"

> "Rest when you're weary. Refresh and renew yourself, your body, your mind, your spirit. Then get back to work."
>
> —**RALPH MARSTON**

To recognize employees of the month, management at **Kentucky Fried Chicken**, owned by Yum Brands, in Louisville, Kentucky, has volunteer employees bring in musical instruments to serenade the achievers. The motley crew of random performers crowd into the employee's cubicle to play "Louie, Louie," or some similar tune. The response has been so favorable, a string quartet was hired to acknowledge higher-level achievers.

During a recent canning season, overtime had climbed so high at the **Dole Food Company** plant in Springfield, Oregon, that workers experienced excessively high stress. One technician said, "I couldn't look at another bag of lettuce!" To prevent burnout, manager Donna Lynn Johnson started a kazoo band. At first, the 325 plant employees were skeptical, but they soon got into the spirit, which helped build morale during tough times. **Apple Computer** has also been known to use a kazoo band for spontaneous celebrations.

Toronto, Canada–based **FreshBooks**, a software company, maintains a choir.

Every year, **Kickstarter**, a public benefit business from Brooklyn, New York, sponsors an employee music recital.

At San Francisco–based music app developer **Smule**, workers can bring their instruments to the office for the company's weekly jam sessions.

---

5 Ways to Have Fun with Art at Work

1. Adopt a funny group mascot and create silly videos featuring it.

2. Make a new-hire video. Have a janitor give the mission/vision/product overview.

3. Watch a movie on Friday afternoon in the conference room.

4. Have an ad hoc team paint a mural on office wall/create other kind of art.

5. Start a work rock band to perform vintage songs at company events.

At the New York City offices of **Spotify**, the digital music service, workers formed a company "house" band. "People want to be able to practice their drums during work hours or learn how to do Pro Tools or record some tracks," says Sandy Smallens, the company's director of artistic marketing and original content.

 Tip

Install a music system in the lunch/break rooms and ask workers to create playlists.

Jellyvision, the employee communication software company based in Chicago, sources its entertainment for company events from within—with about 40 employees coming together to form a jam band.

CASE STUDY

REVERB.COM MUSIC REVIVAL RIVALS WOODSTOCK?

Reverb.com, a marketplace for musical equipment and instruments, also has a team full of musicians and music lovers. "Each year, workers form bands and perform at the company's annual holiday party, covering hits from multiple musical eras," says PR and communications manager Heather Farr Edwards.

Recently, 31 bands exclusively made up of Reverb employees took the stage at Lincoln Hall in Chicago, Illinois, to perform three sets of music. Artists the Reverbers channeled included the following:

- Queen
- David Bowie
- Arcade Fire
- The Jackson 5
- Paramore
- Led Zeppelin
- Blink-182
- Iron Maiden

Other highlights included a flute-backed opera performance, a No Doubt tune complete with brass section, and CEO David Kalt's take on "London Calling" by The Clash.

Syracuse, New York–based **Cxtec**, a technology infrastructure provider, has an in-house rock and roll band called the Cxtec Dinosaurs. Workers pursue their personal music interests and play charitable and customer gigs.

AOL, the online service provider headquartered in New York, is known for their classic employee lip-sync battles. And San Francisco, California–based **Kimpton Hotels** has impromptu dance parties.

Using Google Hangouts with their remote employees, **Incubeta**, the Cape Town, South Africa–based marketing service firm, hosts a daily five-minute afternoon dance party with a dedicated Spotify playlist.

> "Art, freedom, and creativity will change society faster than politics."
>
> —**VICTOR PINCHUK**

Employees at **Cooley**, the nationwide law firm based in Palo Alto, California, rave about their work culture where karaoke matters as much as contracts, and where lawyers take time off to accompany underprivileged kids to Disneyland. New attorneys in some offices of **Perkins Coie** law firm, headquartered in Seattle, Washington, are asked to write and perform skits. They ensure the most ridiculous roles are reserved for managing partners.

"[We] go to the movies," says Suzanne Smith, of **Social Impact Architects** in Dallas, Texas, "to give our team a change of scenery and build the bonds between us." The authors have been known to take their staffs to the opening release of hit action films such as *Jurassic Park*. Of course, the outing was officially listed as a paleontology workshop.

Taking it one step further is **Utility Concierge** of Dallas, Texas, which shot a video spoof of "Happy" by Pharrell Williams. Props included fedoras, scooters, and superhero costumes. They shot footage of staff and their families in various Dallas landmarks. "We posted the clip to our social media accounts and started laughing all over again," says CEO Gabe Abshire. "Making a spoof video may not sound very corporate, but filming one definitely brought our team together—and made everyone from employees to clients and partners smile!"

Who knows **Johnsonville** food products better than the people who make them? Management at the sausage company in Sheboygan Falls, Wisconsin, asked their workers to create the company's TV commercials. After selecting three of the best and wildest suggestions, management had their contributors work on the set, where their scripts were turned into reality.

For many Silicon Valley businesses, *Star Wars* movie screenings have been a relatively low-cost but very effective way to reward high performance. The demand is especially high among techies, who look to the film as inspiration for what to build next. That's why event planners at tech companies have thrown Star Wars parties and rented out theaters for private screenings. And May 4th ("May the Force") is celebrated as Star Wars Day at **Qualcomm** headquarters in San Diego, California. "Star Wars is fun because it connects different types of people. It connects different generations," says Kai Fortney, director of

> "The work of art is a scream of freedom."
>
> —CHRISTO

4 More Ways to Have Fun with Art at Work

1. Do skits to show the importance of company vision/values.

2. Have a weekly podcast/intranet radio station to air funny news.

3. Have a karaoke contest with managers as contestants and employees as judges.

4. Play an uplifting "song of the day" loudly at a set time in the afternoon.

marketing at **Hired**, a popular recruitment start-up in San Francisco. Companies taking advantage of this film franchise include **LinkedIn**, **Lyft**, and **Red Sky Solutions**. Down south in Hawthorne, California, **SpaceX** founder and CEO Elon Musk treats his workers to screenings of other space-related movies such as *Gravity* and *The Martian*.

Commvault, a data protection and management software company based in Tinton Falls, New Jersey, invited workers from around the world to submit photos of life at the company. "We collected a whopping 3,000 photos," says Jesper Helt, vice president and chief human resources officer. To coincide with Employee Appreciation Day, they placed the images into a mosaic that lives as artwork in their offices around the globe. Workers are encouraged to stop by the mosaic sites during the day to place photographs and help with assembly in their local offices.

An employee from **Cleverbridge**, an e-commerce optimization company headquartered in Cologne, Germany, decided to host an instructor-led paint night at the office, and she played the role of the guide. She was so excited, she even prepared her composition at home. "I love that she was able to share her passion for art with us in such an engaging and vulnerable way," says Laura Winegardner, the company's employee experience manager. "It felt so special to see how much joy she experienced simply being able to do something like this at work."

CHAPTER 14

Celebrations, Birthdays & Anniversaries

The more you praise and celebrate your life,
the more there is in life to celebrate.

—OPRAH WINFREY

There are many events throughout the year that allow companies to thank and acknowledge their employees, and fun is a staple at most of these events. These events range from set holidays to company celebrations for success, but they also include individual celebrations that have traditionally been done in most workplaces, such as employee birthdays, work anniversaries, or departures. Although the best forms of recognition are based on an employee's performance, not just their presence at work, any activities where you can make employees feel valued are worth doing.

In a global survey of more than 700 business executives by Harvard Business Review Analytic Services, 93 percent of the respondents say their organizations place a priority on hosting events, including 57 percent who give it a high priority. According to EventMB, guests attend corporate events for networking (82 percent), learning (71 percent), and entertainment (38 percent). Self-improvement is important to 37 percent, and time out of the office is appealing to 16 percent.

Galvanize conducted a survey and found that just over 57 percent of the respondents celebrate the holidays at an off-site holiday party; 19 percent embark on a team outing, 11 percent celebrate at work, and 10 percent don't celebrate with coworkers at all.

Milestone events such as employee anniversaries can serve as a time for employees to reflect on their accomplishments and growth. Fifty percent of the employees surveyed view work anniversaries as a time of reflection, a time to re-evaluate/renew commitment to the company, according to Globoforce, and 74 percent of the employees surveyed who had not celebrated accomplishments with their coworkers said they were more likely to leave their jobs.

Although 82 percent of employees say they would feel good if people noticed and congratulated them for a first work anniversary, only 36 percent say an anniversary made them feel more valued, according to Globoforce.

Receiving a little bit of extra attention on your birthday from your employer and coworkers makes you feel cared for and part of a team. This promotes happiness and reduces stress and burnout. Happy employees are 12 percent to 20 percent more productive than their unhappy counterparts, according to research by the Social Market Foundation and University of Warwick's Centre for Competitive Advantage in the Global Economy.

Some words of caution about end-of-year holiday celebrations: More and more people prefer to opt out of events during this time of year because of feelings of cultural exclusion and fatigue. Remember to apply the Fun principle—Make it safe and fun for everyone. The best bet is to be as inclusive as possible. Here are five guidelines to help you plan such holiday events:

1. The extent and level of celebration of cultural holidays should match the demographic makeup of your organization.

2. Acknowledge the celebration through company-wide communications, and give celebrating workers time off or other ways to mark the holiday.

3. When employees want to share their holidays with the organization, support them with a budget, time to prepare, and acknowledgement of efforts made.

4. Avoid putting a Western spin on holidays from other cultures.

5. Make it safe for anyone to opt out of activities.

Let's explore some of the ways companies call out special occasions with their workers.

Quip, a collaborative productivity software firm headquartered in San Francisco, California, holds an annual holiday cookie cook-off. Employees bake and bring in cookies to share with coworkers and compete in categories including Most Millennial Cookie, Best Non-Cookie Cookie, and Grand Champion Cookie. More important than the baking and voting, everyone looks forward to eating the cookies, and socializing with coworkers across the company.

> "Regardless of what dreams you have, work very hard, play very hard, and have fun."
>
> —JOHN GRUNSFELD

4moms, a better-baby-products provider from Pittsburgh, Pennsylvania, divides its team into different groups. Each group is given a modest budget and asked to create a fun, festive holiday space in the office.

TINYpulse, the Seattle, Washington–based employee engagement software firm, decided years ago to host holiday parties *after* the holidays ended. Now employees can enjoy all the offerings without having to leave for other holiday functions. **OppLoans**, a Chicago-based online lender and service provider, has the same strategy, hosting their holiday party in February.

FlexJobs, the freelance and flex positions company in Boulder, Colorado, manages a virtual gift exchange for their remote workforce. They use Elfster.com to randomly assign Secret Santas.

In Chicago, Illinois, **ParkWhiz**, a parking technology company, celebrated the holidays by giving back. The team organized a coat drive with Button & Zipper to donate winter wear to the needy. They also acted as elves, working with Children's Home & Aid to give presents to disadvantaged families. Just across the windy city, **Echo Global Logistics** also focuses on giving back, with employees donating essential items and gifts to local charities. Down south in Austin, Texas, **Blackbaud** operates an Operation Blue Santa toy drive. Employees at **Kendra Scott** donated 100 percent of their holiday event proceeds to Toys for Tots.

Pampered Chef, the Addison, Illinois–based e-commerce company, hosts a week of holiday events. "We kicked things off with a build-your-own-hot-chocolate bar complete with whipped cream, chocolate syrup, caramel, plain and chocolate chip marshmallows, and more," says talent partner Carolyn Grant. "Tuesday was an afternoon happy hour with trivia, and Wednesday we hosted a delicious holiday lunch complete with mini donuts for dessert and raffle prizes. We ended the week with ugly sweater and

10 Generic Holiday/ Event Ideas

1. Diverse food options
2. Nonspecific décor
3. Potlucks
4. Food truck feast
5. Family/significant other day at the office
6. Holiday health fair
7. Charades
8. Pictionary
9. Conversation bingo
10. Name the tune

pod decorating contests." Boston, Massachusetts–based **Wellframe**, a provider of health management solutions, does something similar with Flannel Friday, Sports-Themed Monday, Wacky Sock Tuesday, and Ugly Sweater Wednesday.

The "Play Patrol" committee of **Mattel Canada Inc.**, the toy manufacturer located in Mississauga, Ontario, organizes social activities such as Valentine's Day archery.

One year, Lynn Theodoro and her team at **Xerox**, the document management company located in Norwalk, Connecticut, met virtually to observe the start of summer. They "went" to a beach—a JibJab animation with coworkers' faces superimposed on cartoon characters who were sunbathing, swimming, and surfing.

Every summer, workers of **The Standard**, a boutique hotel chain, enjoy pool parties at its Los Angeles location, paddle boarding and sunrise yoga at its Miami location, and beer garden visits and poetry readings at its New York City hotels.

Of course, sports tournaments are extremely popular during summer months. **Mutual Mobile**, a technology agency based in Austin, Texas, hosts beach volleyball competitions; Lincoln, Nebraska–based **Hudl**, an online communication platform for coaches and athletes, has the Hudl Open golf tourney; and **Core Digital Media**, a direct response marketing firm from the greater Los Angeles, California, area, has kickball and dodgeball contests.

CASE STUDY

LAKELAND REGIONAL HEALTH HAS FUN AT WORK WEEKS

In the healthcare industry, it is important to balance the seriousness of the culture with some planned fun. This Lakeland, Florida, healthcare system offers a dedicated program called Fun at Work Weeks several times throughout the year.

The LRH Fun Force is led by team members and helps plan several organization-wide activities. The force is committed to encouraging team members to have appropriate Fun at Work within their departments.

To support company "Promises" and foster fun at work, the following Fun at Work Weeks schedule was developed to nurture and inspire the planning of fun within each department. It is suggested that team members and leaders identify appropriate fun and social activities they can enjoy with all of their colleagues and best friends at work during one or two days of the designated Fun at Work Weeks.

Fun at Work Weeks Schedule

March	May	August	November
4th Week, or 1st Week of April	Healthcare Week	2nd Week	2nd Week

The Fun Force has assembled a Fun at Work sample list of possible activities that could be organized within a department or work location. This list provides suggestions and is not all-inclusive. "Team members can identify and plan appropriate Fun at Work activities that are of most interest to their teammates, and do them whenever they desire throughout the year!" says Scott Dimmick, senior vice president/chief HR officer.

Fun at Work Sample List

Team Member Photo Wall

Crazy Sock Day

Bring Your Favorite Toys @ Work

Yoga on Breaks and/or
Laughter Yoga Sessions

Department/Organization
Trivia or Jeopardy Game

Inter or Intra Department
Competitions

Name That Staff Member

Nerf Wars

Price Is Right (Medical Supplies)

Talent Show

Decorate the Workplace Theme

Scavenger Hunt

Favorite Sports Team Theme

Favorite Thing Theme

Simulated Sports Tournaments

Make Me Laugh Contest

Build a Wall of Fame

Create a Humor Bulletin Board

Create a "Bucket List" Bulletin Board

Create Art Together

Favorite Pet Pictures Bulletin Board

Favorite Family Pictures
Bulletin Board

Share Your Favorite Music

Office Exercise Challenge

Establish a 7-Day Happiness
Challenge

Bring Your Favorite Board
Game and Have Game Day

Compliments Competition

Funny Dress Code Day

Always Behavior Challenge

Treasure, Nurture, Inspire
Competition

Department Goals Pictionary

Create Games for the Company
Values (Promises)

Meet, Mix, and Mingle with
Another Department

3 × 3 Mini-Basketball Tournament
between Departments

Conference Table Ice-Curling

Chili Cook-Off Contest

Themed Food Fest

Water Balloon Toss

Formlabs, the 3D printer company based in Boston, Massachusetts, sponsors an annual Tough Mudder Run on Mount Snow and transports the whole company to a camp retreat in the Berkshires.

Balsam Brands, the Redwood City, California–based e-commerce home décor retailer, has a Christmas in July dinner for all employees and their significant others. One year, the party was held on a dinner cruise in San Francisco Bay; another year, they attended a Giants game.

N2 Publishing, located in Wilmington, North Carolina, hosts an annual field day, which consists of tug-of-war, dizzy bat, and a dunk tank. CEO Duane Hixon gives himself permission to have fun and encourages his workers to give themselves permission as well. During field day, Hixon goes out of his way to make himself vulnerable for charity. In this case, he makes his body available as a target. Each time the target is hit, he donates money to a charity that fights human trafficking. One year he dressed as the company mascot, Koala T. Bear, and encouraged workers to slingshot tomatoes at him. "If you hit him in the head, he gave $1,000 to charity. If you hit him on the body, it was $500," says Katherine Daniel, director of people operations. "He's playful and competitive, which is fun for our team, but it's nice to know there's a big-picture element to it," adds Daniel. Over a two-year period, the company donated $50,000 as a result of field days, much of which was due to attacks on the CEO.

7 Tips for Successful Events

1. Create diverse planning committee.
2. Survey cross section of workforce for ideas.
3. Create awareness of other religions.
4. Consider floating holidays and nonstandard dates for events.
5. Make voluntary. Make it safe to opt out.
6. Offer diverse food/drink options and alternatives to alcohol.
7. Offer designated drivers/Uber, Lyft, etc.

Kevin Sheridan, author of *Building a Magnetic Culture* and former president of **HR Solutions**, shares a fun tradition with one of his clients, **Radio Flyer**. Throughout October, employees can dress up for Halloween any day of the month. And everyone can make up their own job titles.

———

Glenn Adams, an executive partner for **Holland & Knight** in Orlando, Florida, oversees 55 lawyers. Each year, Adams encourages attorneys to host in-office Halloween candy giveaways for children in need, and he has his office staff dress in similar themes, from *Gilligan's Island* to *The Beverly Hillbillies*.

> "If you want to celebrate a happy occasion, do it by helping those who are in need."
>
> —**MOHITH AGADI**

———

At **Southwest Airlines**' company-wide Halloween parties, employees—and their families—are encouraged to wear costumes to work for trick-or-treating throughout the office.

———

The Walt Disney Company Halloween celebration is now an over-two-decade tradition. One year, more than 2,000 employees enjoyed music, games, Disney characters, photo locations, food, and a pumpkin patch. And in the "spirit" of giving, all proceeds from the sale of pumpkins were donated to the Burbank, California, YMCA in support of its youth programs. The big event was the costume contest. Over 100 workers competed in one of four categories, including best Disney costume. The C-suite served as judges and selected the winners. Top prizes included one-night stays at a Disneyland Resort hotel.

———

"One company I spoke with likes to take random afternoons off so everyone can participate in fun events," says Michael Canic, president of **Making Strategy Happen**, based in Denver, Colorado. "One afternoon's event—I'm not joking—was an axe-throwing and beer event. It's all fun-and-games until somebody loses a head!"

For an annual employment law conference, **The Employers' Association** in Maumee, Ohio, chose the theme It's a Jungle Out There. After considering the theme, "Judi ran down the hall, bursting into my office, out of breath and eyes wide," says Terry Vernier, the association's seminar learning manager. "She blurted, 'We need *animals* at the ELC!' Then she followed up with, 'They don't have to be tigers or anything.' She was incredibly excited, and it was so *out there* that we decided, why not? What was the harm in exploring this a little bit?" Judi called the Toledo Zoo to explore the idea, and Vernier called the Hilton Garden Inn to find out *if* it could be done. Everything was approved.

> "Material things don't matter if your heart don't get that patter—in your bones."
>
> **—ALLEE WILLIS AND MAURICE WHITE**

On the morning of the conference, the zoo brought in an eagle, an owl, a small alligator, a large snake, and a "cute-as-heck" Mexican hairy dwarf porcupine. The hotel let the association put the animals and caretakers in a meeting room while conference guests were in the opening session. They kept the presence of the animals a secret from attendees until the end of the opening session, when they announced there were *live animals* across the hall to visit. "It was fun to watch attendees' reactions as they made their way into the room with the animals, and I can still see the look on Judi's face when she flew into my office with her proclamation that we *needed* animals at the event. We do really make it a point to have fun during our work days, and the fact that Judi felt comfortable enough to come up with such an out-of-the-blue idea, and then bring it to fruition, is a great illustration of how cool the results can be if you're ok to be a bit playful at work."

Sandra Estrada, founder and owner of Carlsbad, California–based **Employees HME**, sends a monthly fun workplace holiday calendar to clients, prospects, and contacts. "I don't make this calendar, I take it from the internet (see: http://www.successories .com), and I have received great comments about it being a fun way to engage with the employees," says Estrada. For example, "Did you know that September 21–27 is the International Week of Happiness at Work? You can pick any holiday that you would like to celebrate with your employees and make something fun of it."

At **OOPS!**, a specialty store in Providence, Rhode Island, employees choose offbeat "holidays" to celebrate, such as National Hug Month or Willie Nelson's birthday. Employees dress to fit the occasion and have a great time, and it costs the store nothing.

A Boston-based biotech company held a Ferris Bueller Day Off. Under a guise of a strategic planning meeting, all staff was summoned to the company's auditorium. The CEO came out in a bathrobe and told employees that while they had had a successful year, he worried that everyone was working too hard,

> **9 Uncommon Holidays to Celebrate at Work**
>
> 1. National Belly Laugh Day, January 24
> 2. Fun at Work Day, January 26
> 3. National Pi (3.1416 . . .) Day, March 14
> 4. Take Your Sons and Daughters to Work Day, April 26
> 5. May the Fourth Be with You (*Star Wars* debut), May 4
> 6. National Doughnut Day, June 1
> 7. International Week of Happiness at Work
> 8. Bring Your Parents to Work Day, November 4
> 9. Bring Your (create your own) to Work Day, TBD

5 Retirement Party Ideas

1. Invite family and friends.

2. Have a theme:
   - *This Is Your Life*–style TV show (put online)
   - Roast
   - Geography party (if they're moving)
   - Costume party
   - Retiree's hobbies
   - Have out of office—museum, park, beach, lake/river/mountains

3. Make it for charity.

4. Encourage guest stories.

5. Include popular music playlist.

"The meaning of life is not celebrating your birth, it is celebrating your work."

—AMIT KALANTRI

saying it was important to have balance, and he proclaimed the rest of the day off, wheeled in popcorn and drinks, and showed the movie to the company! He asked everyone to plan to take another bonus day off when they felt they needed it in the upcoming year.

***

Nutanix, a cloud computing company headquartered in San Jose, California, celebrates Lunar New Year, and on the lighter side, they observe National Scrabble Day.

***

For over two decades, **The Container Store**, a storage and organization company based in Coppell, Texas, has hosted an annual chili cook-off. Each department chooses a theme and builds a booth to reflect it. They even dress up in costumes to complete the effect.

***

On January 28, as part of Have Fun at Work Day, 2,000 employees at the **University of Washington** in Seattle got together to rehearse for a chance to set the Guinness World Record for world's largest umbrella dance—a choreographed, synchronized umbrella dance that must be on video for five minutes.

***

Chatmeter, a brand management company based in San Diego, California, uses Employee Appreciation Day to celebrate their best team wins and favorite off-the-job activities. During the week before Appreciation Day, they have a social media contest for employees to post favorite pictures from past company events, with captions naming ideas for what to do next.

***

San Francisco, California–headquartered **Kimpton Hotels and Restaurants** host a Housekeeping Appreciation Week. Included are days devoted to stacks of pancakes, spa treatments, and games—perhaps the most favorite: toilet-papering the general manager's office.

FreshBooks is a Toronto, Canada–based, cloud-based accounting software company where Fun is a core value. Once a year, the firm rents a children's camp for all workers and their families—dogs too—to enjoy.

The Happiness Crew at **Zoom Video Communications** based in San Jose, California, coordinates events like Bring Your Parent to Work Day, Bring Your Kid to Work Day, Zoom Olympics, and happy hours. At **Workday**, a cloud-based HR and finance software provider headquartered in Pleasanton, California, workers proudly bring mom and dad to Bring Your Parents to Workday.

Toast, the cloud-based restaurant software company headquartered in Boston, Massachusetts, split its workforce into teams, and each one had mystery dinners with 23 of their Boston-area clients. Then the whole company met at one of their clients' nightclubs to mingle and share stories.

WillowTree LLC, an IT firm based in Charlottesville, Virginia, hosts two large company-wide parties annually; company-sponsored sports teams (e.g., kickball, softball, curling); video game nights; movie

10 Ways to Celebrate Thanksgiving at Work

1. Potluck/international cuisine
2. Cooking contest
3. Recipe/pie swap
4. Tailgate party
5. Food/charitable drive; volunteer on project
6. Gratitude wall; say "Thanks" walk around/ notes exchange
7. Parade/walk or hike
8. Thanksgiving "mishaps" storytelling
9. "Two truths and a lie" game
10. Bowling with pumpkins

nights; board game nights; company band practices; and other events that appeal to a variety of worker interests.

Recently, **Mood Media** (aka Muzak), an in-store music company based in Austin, Texas, surprised its staff with a live performance by The Spazmatics, a popular 1980s new wave rock show. Company executives came dressed as '80s rock stars.

Camden Property Trust, a multifamily property development and management company based in Houston, Texas, offers monthly activities like team trivia and Pinewood Derby car racing. They also have a Crazy Sock Day.

Bamboo HR, the human resources software company located in Lindon, Utah, gives employees their birthdays off, encouraging them to spend the day with family and friends, or doing what they love to do.

At **Blazer Industries**, a modular building manufacturer in Aumsville, Oregon, the Older Than Dirt Club puts a leafless tree on people's desks in honor of their 50th birthdays.

At Tampa, Florida, money-transfer service **Transfer-Wise**, workers get their birthdays off and receive two movie-ticket vouchers for a film of their choice.

"I like to surprise my contractors with something creative," says James Heidebrecht of **Policy Architects**, a firm located in Toronto, Canada. "The latest present

[I gave] was a spa package for one of my writers. She's a mom that works from home, and I thought she could use some 'me' time. It really meant a lot to her that I made the extra effort to think of something she might like. With so many options online, there's really no excuse. Nowadays, you can send a Send-OutCard, a gift basket, flowers, movie passes, even legendary pizza from Chicago or New York."

At **Groupon**, an e-commerce marketplace headquartered in Chicago, Illinois, every worker gets a bright green Adidas track jacket on their one-year anniversary. The jacket has the person's name or nickname and the company's logo on it. For every year thereafter, the employee gets to add a star.

"Faceversaries" are a big part of **Facebook**'s company culture. They shower employees with festive balloons and post heartfelt wishes on the platform itself, which encourages both friends and colleagues to participate in the celebration.

When Bob Vaughn retired from **Lakeland Community College** as dean of business, virtually no one realized he sang and played the piano. During the formal retirement presentation, Bob asked the stage manager to pull back the curtain, revealing a piano and a microphone. He proceeded to perform five parodies he'd written covering roof repair, interminable meetings, and the National Education Association. People laughed and recalled his presentation years after his retirement.

10 Ways to Celebrate Work Anniversaries

1. E-card signed by all
2. Interrupt their daily routine
3. Feature on website landing page
4. Bake cake
5. Customize a gift
6. Lunch w/ CEO or president
7. Limo ride to office/ special parking space
8. Sponsor an outside experience
9. Contribute to charity
10. Paid time off

CHAPTER 15

Charities & Volunteering

I've learned that you shouldn't go through life with a catcher's mitt on
both hands; you need to be able to throw something back.

—MAYA ANGELOU

Another easy area for companies to support employees in having fun together is through charities and volunteering. This provides employees a chance to meet others in the organization they may not typically work with and to get to know each other through non-work activities, building relationships that are stronger and better apt to handle challenging situations that arise at work.

Participating with any charity also helps employees to feel better about themselves and thus better about their organization that supported them in the activity. These types of experiences can lift us out of our daily routines and expand our perspective, allowing us to meet other interesting people and do work for a greater good. For example, Mario and Bob have had a lot of fun pounding nails to help build houses for the homeless on weekends for Habitat for Humanity.

Most companies support charities for their employees, and most employees think more of their company for doing so. According to Nonprofits Source, 86 percent of companies believe that employees expect them to provide opportunities to engage in the community, 87 percent believe their employees expect them to support causes and issues that matter to those employees, 78 percent of Americans want companies to address social justice issues, and 88 percent of Millennials find their job more fulfilling when they have opportunities to make a positive impact on society and the environment.

The Cone Communications Employee Engagement Study found 55 percent of employees would choose to work for a socially responsible company, even if it meant a lower salary.

America's Charities' Snapshot Employer Research found 82 percent of the survey respondents say employees want the opportunity to volunteer with peers in a corporate-supported event.

According to Nonprofits Source, more than half of U.S. employers maintain the tradition of donating to nonprofit entities and programs. Approximately $5 billion is raised through workplace giving annually, an estimated $2 to $3 billion is donated through matching gift programs annually, which 9 out of 10 companies offer. An estimated $6 to $10 billion in matching gift funds goes unclaimed per year, 79 percent of companies reported increased donor participation rates, and 73 percent raised more money. Employees who engaged in corporate giving programs tended to have 75 percent longer tenures with the company.

> "Volunteers do not necessarily have the time; they just have the heart."
>
> **—ELIZABETH ANDREW**

As mentioned by the National Philanthropic Trust, approximately 77 million Americans—30 percent of the adult population—volunteer their time, talents, and energy to making a difference. And 75 percent of U.S. adults feel physically healthier by volunteering. The mental and emotional benefits of volunteering are even greater, with 93 percent reporting an improved mood, 79 percent reporting lower stress levels, and 88 percent reporting increased self-esteem by giving back.

Also mentioned by Nonprofits Source, nearly 60 percent of companies offer paid time off for employees to volunteer, and an average of 30 percent of employees volunteer. People who volunteer report that they feel better emotionally, mentally, and physically.

Supporting charities, matching employee donations, and allowing employees to volunteer for their favorite charities make for a more socially responsible employer. It's the right thing to do and employees feel good working for a company that supports such endeavors.

Every quarter, **Cupertino Electric Inc.**, headquartered in San Jose, California, organizes an activity to bring employees together to volunteer their services for a cause.

> "Have fun. The game is a lot more enjoyable when you're trying to do more than just make money."
>
> —TONY HSIEH

Through its Nitro Gives initiative, **Nitro Software Inc.**, a San Francisco, California, firm takes employees to the beach for a fun time of cleaning up.

DISC, a printing and packaging business located in Hauppauge, New York, helps employees have fun by supporting a blood drive twice a year and annual participation in the Long Island Cares Summer Food Drive and Walk MS: Long Island.

Omaha, Nebraska–based custom software company **Aviture** donates a portion of its profits to charities and encourages workers to do the same. Their Aspire program teaches STEM principles to 7th- to 12th-grade students in The Garage, a large physically open space within Aviture. It's an incubator to spark innovation in the local community. Guest speakers come in, start-ups get general guidance, and investors are connected with entrepreneurs.

Each year **Kimpton Hotels**, a San Francisco, California–based hotel and restaurant brand, joins forces with Chefs Cycle, a fundraising endurance event from Washington, D.C., to raise funds and awareness for their partner, No Kid Hungry, a nonprofit also located in D.C. Its team of chefs, hotel staff, and top execs have fun together bicycling 300 miles to combat childhood hunger in the U.S.

Based in Santa Monica, California, **VideoAmp**, an advertising service, celebrates the holidays by giving back. A few years ago, VideoAmp was a tiny company with 17 employees who all shared a commitment to helping people. VideoAmp Gives Back! started off simple. At first, it worked with organizations like the Salvation Army. Over time, it chose to do everything in-house for charities: from lunch kits, hygiene products, and toy drives to sponsoring families' Christmases. All events were recommended by employees, and as the company grew, so did the impact of the VideoAmp Gives Back! program.

Profitero, a Dublin, Ireland–based e-commerce analytics platform, partners with **United Way**, a nonprofit organization based in Alexandria, Virginia, to help families who can't afford to buy holiday gifts for their children. Workers break into teams, buy gifts on their lists, and return to the office to wrap them. It's a great team-building experience with competition and trash talk over which team wraps the best.

TripAdvisor, the free travel guide and research website, headquartered in Needham, Massachusetts, supports employee giving and volunteerism throughout the year. Through their annual summertime Global Volunteer Month, all TripAdvisor Media Group (TAMG) offices and subsidiary companies meet to help support their local communities.

4 Ways to Be Charitable at Work

1. Host fun quarterly potluck lunch. Charge small fee and donate proceeds to charity.

2. Choose a charity and host a fundraising event such as casino night.

3. Have workers pick a charity that company will donate money to at year's end.

4. Encourage workers to volunteer with a charity on company time.

Projects range from school and shelter renovations, to workforce development workshops, to providing nutritious meals.

Camden Property Trust, the real estate investment trust headquartered in Houston, Texas, pays for employees to leave work to volunteer with their local Habitat for Humanity, Make-A-Wish Foundation, and

CASE STUDY

WARBY PARKER HAS ITS EYES ON CHARITIES AND VOLUNTEERING

Warby Parker (WP), the vision and optical products company based in New York City, knows that 2.5 billion people around the globe need glasses but cannot get them. Of these, 624 million cannot learn or work because of their visual impairments.

Through its Buy a Pair, Give a Pair program, WP partners with organizations worldwide to ensure that for every pair of glasses purchased, a pair of glasses is sent to someone in need.

WP has two strategies to get glasses into the right hands:

1. Training adults to administer basic eye exams and sell glasses at ultra-affordable prices.

2. Directly giving vision care and glasses to school-age children in their classrooms.

WP has supported its partner, VisionSpring, with its social entrepreneurship model internationally. Low-income men and women get and sell radically affordable eyeglasses, earn a living, and care for their families. In addition to getting vocational training, this model makes eyecare significantly more accessible for people with few or no options. Over half of VisionSpring's customers are getting glasses for the first time.

food banks. Similarly, at **Zoom Video Communications**, along with volunteering for events to support Habitat for Humanity, the Special Olympics, and the MS Society, workers strive to win their own Yellow Rubber Duck. This prestigious award is bestowed upon all employees who volunteer for a Zoom event that supports a charity.

> "You have to be a place that's more than a paycheck for people."
>
> **—RICK FEDERICO**

According to the Centers for Disease Control and Prevention, in the United States, vision disability is the single most prevalent disabling condition among children. Through its Pupils Project, WP partners with organizations and local government agencies like the Department of Education in New York City and the Department of Health in Baltimore, Maryland. It gives free vision screenings, eye exams, and glasses to schoolchildren—in their classrooms. In Mexico, WP supports an organization, Ver Bien, that uses a similar school-based model.

"We give our employees a couple of paid volunteer days to go into these schools and help out however they can, whether it's related to glasses and vision or not," says WP cofounder Dave Gilboa. The company fully supports workers' efforts with time off or money so they can see the positive impact they're making. It also gives funds to the staffs of each store to donate to local organizations when they hit key sales targets.

During Hurricane Harvey, WP didn't bat an eye but went into immediate action to help victims. "Our (new) store there was fine, but instead of having a grand-opening celebration," says Gilboa, "we paid for our employees to volunteer for a month at local organizations."

The 521-room **Holiday Inn** Chicago-Mart Plaza is involved with 28 community outreach programs. They do everything from serving lunch or baking cookies for families staying at Chicago's Ronald McDonald House, to changing bedding at homeless shelters. They also partner with a local public elementary school.

***

Timberland outdoor apparel retailer, headquartered in Stratham, New Hampshire, pays workers to volunteer for up to 40 hours annually. This paid time-off program is separate from any other personal or vacation time.

***

HVAC.com, a heating, ventilation, and air conditioning company based in Monroe, Ohio, encourages its employees to volunteer with local charities and supports sending some employees on international mission trips.

***

> "Volunteers don't get paid, not because they're worthless, but because they're priceless."
>
> —SHERRY ANDERSON

Mo Anderson, vice chairperson of **Keller Williams**, the world's largest real estate franchise, launched KW Cares, a charity that supports agents and their communities in sudden emergencies and during natural disasters. For example, the aftermath of Hurricane Harvey in 2017 coincided with Keller Williams's annual training in Austin, Texas, which drew associates from around the world. The company transformed its training into a large-scale relief effort, sending 3,000 associates to help in storm-ravaged areas.

***

Healthcare giant **Johnson & Johnson** prides itself on caring for the world, one person at a time. That philosophy translates into encouraging workers to volunteer. Eligible individuals take up to two weeks off—one fully paid—to volunteer for a nonprofit of their choice each year. For example, Reinhard Juraschek, Ph.D., associate director of research & development at Ethicon, goes to Guatemala as a volunteer with Rotary International's Iowa MOST (Miles of Smiles Team) to perform cleft lip and palate surgeries on children. "It's so rewarding," says Juraschek. "This was a way to do something with my skills and background that was completely, undoubtedly good."

> "As you grow older, you will discover you have two hands—one for helping yourself, the other for helping others."
>
> —**AUDREY HEPBURN**

Goldman Sachs, the financial giant based in New York City, hosts a fun, all-night scavenger hunt in the city. Described by the *Atlantic* as "part performance art, part nerd Olympics, and part urban scavenger hunt," it has raised more than a million dollars in a single evening.

New York City–based **Deloitte**, a professional services firm, offers three to six months of partially paid leave for workers to volunteer or pursue career-enhancing opportunities.

> "Be happy when you work, thankful when you earn, cautious when you spend, shrewd when you save, and charitable when you give."
>
> —**MATSHONA DHLIWAYO**

Salesforce, the cloud computing company headquartered in San Francisco, California, calls its integrated philanthropic approach the "1-1-1" model. The company donates 1 percent of its software, 1 percent of its equity, and 1 percent of its workers' time to deserving causes. They have contributed more than $240 million in grants, 3.5 million hours of community service, and product donations to more than 39,000 nonprofits and education institutions.

Microsoft donates $17 to nonprofits for every hour an employee volunteers his or her time.

Top 4 Types of Organizations to Volunteer With

1. Religious (32 percent)
2. Sport/hobby/cultural/ arts (26 percent)
3. Educational/youth service (19 percent)
4. Civic/political/profes- sional/international (6 percent)

SnackNation, a healthy snack delivery company headquartered in Culver City, California, offers a Clothing Swap program. Started by SnackNation project manager Hannah Avellaneda, clothes are brought to work and traded. Any remaining clothes are donated to a survivor of domestic violence through an organization called Becky's Fund. Says Avellaneda, "It's a lot of fun and a great ice breaker for new employees. It also gives us a good sense of accomplishment and purpose. We are able to give back both internally and to the external community. We get to de-clutter, and we're super appreciative that our hand-me-downs are put to good use."

Through its wellness program, employees of **Earth Friendly Products** can also trade clothes and household items with one another. Additionally, if workers want to trade their cars for more environmentally friendly ones, the company will contribute financially. Plus the company gives $1,000 to every employee who chooses to move closer to the office to cut their carbon footprint.

Conclusion &
Discussion Guide

If you are not having fun at work, do something different.

—LARRY JAMES

We hope that you have found several new fun ideas or approaches to apply for yourself and others in your work. Our premise for this book was simple: We each can impact how much fun we have with our work. It's a matter of (1) choosing to have fun, (2) being open and flexible, (3) experimenting and trying new things, (4) learning from what you try, refining and reapplying those things, and (5) being patient in allowing fun to permeate your group or company.

If you have an example of fun at work you'd like to share for possible inclusion in a future edition of this book, please send it to us at bob@drbobnelson.com or mario@tamayogroup.com. If you'd like to find out more about any example used in this book, contact us for that as well.

This book may have also sparked some of your own ideas and raised questions that would be beneficial to explore with others with whom you work. The following items are discussion questions you might find helpful to explore with others at the individual, leader, team, and organizational levels.

Individual

1. What does it mean for you to have "fun"?

2. What is your Fun story; that is, what or who has shaped your view of this topic?

3. What can you personally do to ensure more fun happens for yourself and others at work?

4. What narratives, cultural scripts have you learned about having fun at work?

5. What characteristics about fun have you internalized as norms?

6. How can you influence others you work with to have more fun at work?

7. How might you be complicit in not having fun at work (silence, denial, defense)? To what extent do you recognize/praise yourself and others for having fun at work?

Leader

1. Have you ever discussed the topic of fun with your employees? Could you do that?

2. Do employees feel safe trying fun things at work?

3. How do you ensure all members of your team are included in fun activities?

4. What could you do to "lead the charge" in having your team have more fun?

Team

1. What can your team immediately do to have more fun together?

2. To what extent is the team comfortable talking about having more fun?

3. What is the root cause of your team not having more fun? How can you address that?

4. To what extent is fun encouraged or minimized on your team?

5. Does your current work culture encourage members to have fun?

6. To what extent do you recognize/praise yourself and others for having fun?

Organization

1. To what extent do you have a fun work culture?

2. What is the history of your organization having fun? Was it fun before, but not now? What's the root cause of the change?

3. To what extent does your organization encourage, recognize, and praise workers for having fun?

4. Have you sought employee input about ways to have more fun?

5. Do you have a Fun Committee? Could you start one?

6. Does your organization seek to include everyone in your company in fun activities?

7. Who is involved in making decisions about fun, inclusive policies? Who needs to be involved?

8. Have you sought one or more executives to help sponsor a fun culture?

9. How are organizational leaders encouraged to allow their teams to have more fun?

10. Have you considered making Fun a core value of your organization?

Acknowledgments

Many people work together to get a book created, written, finished, and published. The authors sure had fun doing this book and would like to thank the following people for helping. We hope they all had some fun in the process as well.

Our spouses: Bob's wife, Jennifer, and Mario's wife, Michele, have put up with our antics for too many years to mention, yet they've consistently supported and encouraged us individually and in working together. In addition, Jennifer spent a lot of time on researching, writing, and compiling an initial draft of this book between real jobs over five years ago.

Many researchers helped to find, well . . . research, fun in the workplace and examples of what that specifically looked like for us to include in this book. This included longtime researcher of multiple books for Bob, Jeanie Casison, plus student interns Anna Freeman, Allyson Lee, and Claudia Kayda and their faculty sponsor who recommended them, Michelle Dean, associate professor in the Department of Management for the Fowler College of Business at San Diego State University in San Diego, California.

Several colleagues gave us permission to use content from their books, including Matt Weinstein, author of *Managing to Have Fun*, and Adrian Gostick, author of *The Levity Effect*. Leslie Yerkes, co-author of *301 Ways to Have Fun at Work*, provided previously unpublished examples. We also had original direct submissions for this book from people around the world!

Dozens of people gave us feedback about potential titles for this book, including Harry Paul, co-author of *Fish! A Remarkable Way to Boost Morale and Improve Results*, plus we received reviewer comments and suggestions on an early draft of the manuscript from Amity Bacon, Rachel Henry, and Aspen Baker.

And thanks go to our very talented editor and founder of Berrett-Koehler, Steve Piersanti, who personally worked with the authors, nurturing us through every step of the publishing process, and the other great staff at Berrett-Koehler, who each played an integral role in the creation and marketing of this book, including Jeevan Sivasubramaniam, managing director, editorial; Edward Wade, vice president, design and production; Valerie Caldwell, associate director of design and production; Kristen Frantz, VP of sales & marketing; Katie Sheehan, marketing manager; María Jesús Aguiló, vice president of global and digital sales; and Catherine Lengronne, international sales.

Thank you, one and all!

Featured Companies

Aceable Austin, TX, 96
Drivers' education and defensive driving

Acuity Financial Sheboygan, WI, 38
Financial insurance company

AdExchanger New York, NY, 96
Media and events company

**Administrative Office of the
Courts** Wilmington, DE, 20
Judicial branch

Adobe San Jose, CA, 146, 159
Computer software company

AdventHealth Orlando, FL, 118, 127
Healthcare system

Adventure Architects San Francisco, CA,
129
Corporate retreat experience firm

Advocate Aurora Health Milwaukee, WI,
45
Healthcare system

Airbnb San Francisco, CA, 59, 145
Vacation housing provider

All Star Directories Seattle, WA, 102
Online education service

Amazon Seattle, WA, 61, 113, 166, 167
Technology and retail company

**AAA (American Automobile
Association)** Los Angeles, CA, 48
Federation of motor clubs

Amica Insurance Lincoln, RI, 94
Mutual insurance company

**Amplus Communication Pte
Ltd** Singapore, Singapore, 114
Microwave and millimeter-wave service

Amway Ada Township, MI, 117
Marketing company

AOL New York, NY, 101, 159, 174
Web portal and online service

Apple Inc. Cupertino, CA, 172
Technology company

Aprilaire Madison, WI, 159
Air purifiers and thermostats

Asana Silicon Valley, CA, 59
Web and mobile application

Ask.com Oakland, CA, 141
Question-answering company

Atlassian Sydney, Australia, 97, 120
Software multinational

Automattic San Francisco, CA, 141
Global distributing company

Aviture Omaha, NE, 135, 194
Software development company

Balsam Brands Redwood City, CA, 184
Home décor retailer

BAM Communications San Diego, CA, 167
Media-relations firm

Bamboo HR Lindon, UT, 104, 190
Human resource software

Bank of America Charlotte, NC, 33
Investment bank and financial services

Banker's Trust New York, NY, 123
Banking organization

Baxter International Deerfield, IL, 103
Healthcare company

BC Hydro Vancouver, Canada, 57
Electric services company

Bell Partners Greensboro, NC, 19
Apartment management firm

Belmont University Nashville, TN, 138
Private Christian university

Ben & Jerry's Homemade Holdings Inc. South
Burlington, VT, 162
Manufacturer of ice cream

Berrett-Koehler Publishers Oakland, CA, 18
Independent publisher

Bigcommerce Austin, TX, 101
Technology company

Bitly New York, NY, 65
URL shortening service

Blackbaud Austin, TX, 180
Cloud computing provider

Blazer Industries Aumsville, OR, 190
Construction company

Box Inc. Redwood City, CA, 154
Cloud management service

Brivo Bethesda, MD, 60
Security management software

Buddytruk Santa Monica, CA, 61
App connecting truck owners

Buffer San Francisco, CA, 96
Software application

Business First Louisville, KY, 33
Business newspaper

Business Solutions Inc. The Woodlands, TX, 57
Information system consulting firm

Camden Property Trust Houston, TX, 165, 190,
196
Real estate company

Canon Solutions America Norcross, GA, 125, 156
Integrated systems technology firm

Capital One McLean, VA, 73
Banking company

Carfax Centreville, VA, 83
Vehicle report company

CarGurus East Cambridge, MA, 94
Car-shopping website

CaseWare International Inc. Toronto, Canada,
34
Software solution company

Centene Corporation St. Louis, MO, 23
Healthcare insurer

Chatmeter San Diego, CA, 188
Brand management company

Chevron U.S.A. San Ramon, CA, 77
Energy corporation

Cisco San Jose, CA, 77, 142
Technology conglomerate

ClearCompany Boston, MA, 105
Talent management software

Cleverbridge Cologne, Germany, 176
E-commerce solutions company

Commvault Tinton Falls, NJ, 176
Data protection and management software

Container Store, The Coppell, TX, 109, 188
Retail chain company

Cooley LLP Palo Alto, CA, 174
Law firm

Core Digital Media Playa Vista, CA, 104, 181
Marketing platform

Costco Issaquah, WA, 157
Big-box retailer

CourseHorse New York, NY, 103
Marketplace of classes

Crabtree Group Winchester, TN, 70
Dental practice management

Crowe Chicago, IL, 72
Professional services firm

CultureIQ New York, NY, 69
Culture management company

Cupertino Electric Inc. San Jose, CA, 194
Electrical engineering company

Cvent McLean, VA, 60
Survey software firm

Cxtec Syracuse, NY, 63, 174
Technology infrastructure provider

DeBragga & Spiller Inc. Jersey City, NJ, 28
Wholesale meat and poultry products

DeliveringHappiness.com Las Vegas, NV, 73, 85
Consulting and coaching company

Deloitte Consulting New York, NY, 2, 111, 199
Professional services network

Delta Air Lines Atlanta, GA, 114
Airline company

Department of Economic Security
Phoenix, AZ, 33
State government agency

Digital Equipment Corporation
(now Compaq) Maynard, MA, 118
Computer company

DISC Hauppauge, NY, 194
Printing and packaging company

DISQO Los Angeles, CA, 98
Insights platform

DLF Global San Diego, CA, 19
International shipping and logistics company

Dogtopia Phoenix, AZ, 168
Dog daycare provider

Dole Food Company Springfield, OR, 172
Agricultural corporation

DR Systems (now part of IBM) San Diego, CA, 158
Medical imaging solutions company

Dscout Chicago, IL, 34
Customer insight technology provider

dTelepathy San Diego, CA, 38
User-experience design company

Duluth Trading Co. Belleville, WI, 159
Men and women's workwear

Earth Friendly Products Cypress, CA, 200
Green-powered cleaning products

Echo Global Logistics Chicago, IL, 180
Supply chain management services

EdgeCast Los Angeles, CA, 160
Content delivery network

Employees HME Carlsbad, CA, 187
Human resources consulting firm

Employers' Association, The Maumee, OH, 186
Human resources consulting and training

Enterprise Holdings Surrey, United Kingdom,
32, 69, 83, 157
Car rentals company

Envoy San Francisco, CA, 92
Visitor registration products

Etsy Brooklyn, NY, 153
E-commerce of handmade goods

Eurobank Athens, Greece, 118
Financial organization

Evergage Somerville, MA, 59
Cloud-based software firm

Evernote Redwood City, CA, 39, 51
Note-taking application

Evolution Hospitality San Clemente, CA, 152
Hotel management company

F+B New York New York, NY, 95
Consulting and commercial brokerage

Facebook Menlo Park, CA, 61, 64, 191
Social media conglomerate

FairShare CSA Coalition Madison, WI, 159
Connects customers with farmers

Fareast Mercantile Trade Company Ltd. Lagos, Nigeria, 58
Manufacturing, retail, and exporter

Fast Company New York, NY, 57, 101
Business magazine

FitSmallBusiness New York, NY, 87
Digital resource for businesses

FlexJobs Boulder, CO, 86, 180
Job-search website

FlyHomes Seattle, WA, 165
Real estate agency

Ford Motor Company Dearborn, MI, 87
Automaker

Formlabs Boston, MA, 184
3D printer company

Four Pi Systems (now a part of Hewlett-Packard) San Diego, CA, 111
Manufacturer of test equipment

4moms Pittsburgh, PA, 179
Baby products provider

FreshBooks Toronto, Canada, 172, 189
Software company

FUN.com Mankato, MN, 101
Toy company

Funeral Directors Life Insurance Abilene, TX, 101
Life insurance company

GCL Downers Grove, IL, 105
Logistics company

Genentech San Francisco, CA, 146, 159
Pharmaceuticals pioneer

Genera Games Seville, Spain, 59
Mobile game publisher

General Assembly New York, NY, 83
Education company

General Dynamics Reston, VA, 39, 74
Aerospace and defense corporation

General Mills Minneapolis, MN, 128
Food company

Genetic Synergy Steamboat Springs, CO, 16
Bio-fitness training

Genly Santa Monica, CA, 121
Internet marketing service

GitLab San Francisco, CA, 83, 97
Web-based repository management

Go Canvas Reston, VA, 94
Mobile platform

Go Game, The San Francisco, CA, 129
Team-building production firm

Goldman Sachs New York, NY, 199
Investment bank and financial services

Good-Loop Edinburgh, United Kingdom, 150
Online advertising company

Goodway Group Jenkintown, PA, 95
Digital media firm

Google Mountain View, CA, 72, 101, 150
Multinational technology company

Great Plains Software Fargo, ND, 78
ERP software company

Greene Turtle New York, NY, 112
Restaurant chain

Greenvelope Seattle, WA, 104
Electronic invitations

Groupon Chicago, IL, 191
E-commerce marketplace

Gusto San Francisco, CA, 136
Payroll software business

Hardee's Food Systems St. Louis, MO, 112
Fast-food chain

Harmless Harvest San Francisco, CA, 150
Coconut water company

Help Scout Boston, MA, 94
Global help-desk software

Hennelly & Grossfeld LLP Marina Del Rey, CA, 45
Law firm

Hewlett-Packard Inc. Palo Alto, CA, 111
Technology company

High-Heeled Success Cincinnati, OH, 52
Consulting business

Hilton Hotels & Resorts McLean, VA, 78, 137
Hospitality company

Holiday Inn Chicago, IL, 198
Hotel chain

Holland & Knight Orlando, FL, 185
Law firm

Home Depot Atlanta, GA, 49
Home improvement retailer

Hopper Montreal, Canada, 101
Mobile travel booking app

Horovitz, Rudoy & Rogan Pittsburgh, PA, 136
CPA firm

Houzz Palo Alto, CA, 137
Interior design application firm

HR Solutions Baton Rouge, LA, 125, 185
Human resources management provider

Hubspot Cambridge, MA, 77, 125, 145, 157
Inbound marketing software

Hudl Lincoln, Nebraska, 181
Communication platform for coaches and
athletes

Huge Brooklyn, NY, 94
Global digital company

Hugo San Francisco, CA, 59
Meeting notes developer

Hulu Santa Monica, CA, 63, 151
Subscription video service

Huntington National Bank Akron, Ohio, 117
Bank holding company

Hursthouse Landscape Architects Bolingbrook,
IL, 110
Landscape architect

HVAC.com Monroe, OH, 105, 198
Heating and air conditioning

Hyatt Hotels Corporation Chicago, IL, 89, 113, 160
Multinational hospitality company

Hyland Software Westlake, OH, 38, 100
Software firm

Hyr New York, NY, 39
Connects short-staffed businesses

Image Group, The Holland, OH, 48
Marketing and advertising firm

Incubeta Cape Town, South Africa, 91, 174
Marketing service

Industrial Management Institute Tehran, Iran,
29
Consulting firm and business school

Infor New York, NY, 64
Software company

Ink48 Hotel New York, NY, 105
Leisure hotel

In-N-Out Irvine, CA, 161
Fast-food restaurant chain

Innovid New York, NY, 95
Online advertising technology

Insight Enterprises Sugar Grove, IL, 18
Technology company

**Institute of Electrical and Electronic
Engineers** Hollywood, CA, 15
Professional association

Interos Arlington, VA, 159
Technology start-up

Inuvo Little Rock, AR, 96
Advertising technology firm

Iteris Inc. Santa Ana, CA, 109
Software and consulting service

Jellyvision Chicago, IL, 173
Software company

JLL (Jones Lang LaSalle) Chicago, IL, 96
Global real estate investment

Johnson & Johnson New Brunswick, NJ, 145, 198
Healthcare company

Johnsonville LLC Sheboygan Falls, WI, 175
Sausage company

Jordan Evans Group Cambria, CA, 18
Employee retention and engagement consulting

Just Fearless Los Angeles, CA, 61
Business development consulting

Kaiser Permanente Oakland, CA, 159
Healthcare provider

Keller Williams Austin, TX, 198
Real estate franchise

Ken Blanchard Companies, The Escondido, CA,
56, 60, 75, 119
Leadership development programs

Kendra Scott Austin, TX, 180
Jewelry company

Kentucky Fried Chicken (owned by Yum
Brands) Louisville, KY, 172
Fast-food restaurant chain

Kickstarter Brooklyn, NY, 160, 172
Public benefit corporation

Kimley-Horn Design Raleigh, NC, 50
Planning and design consultation

Kimpton Hotels & Restaurants San Francisco,
CA, 38, 48, 78, 105, 169, 174, 189, 194
Hotel and restaurant brand

KnowBe4 Clearwater, FL, 135
Cybersecurity awareness training

Korry Electronics Everett, WA, 45
Human-machine interface (HMI)

Kroger Cincinnati, OH, 146
Grocery retailer

L.L. Bean Freeport, ME, 153
Outdoor apparel company

Lakeland Community College Kirtland, OH, 191
Community college

Lakeland Regional Health Lakeland, FL, 182
Healthcare system

LaSalle Chicago, IL, 33, 68, 84
Global real estate investment firm

Learn2Appreciate Ontario, Canada, 46
Incentive company

LEGO Billund, Denmark, 135, 152
Plastic brick toy company

Libby Gill Los Angeles, CA, 91
Author, business coach, and brand strategy

LinkedIn Sunnyvale, CA, 129, 176
Employment-oriented service

Liquid Web Lansing, MI, 88
Online hosting company

L'Oreal Clichy, France, 122
Global cosmetics company

Lyft San Francisco, CA, 114, 176
Ride-sharing company

Making Strategy Happen Denver, CO, 82, 186
Consulting firm

Mannix Marketing Glen Falls, NY, 124, 158
Digital marketing company

Marburn Academy New Albany, OH, 84, 171
Private school

March Cambridge, MA, 98
Software company

Maritz Inc. Fenton, MO, 68
Sales and marketing services

Mars Inc. McLean, VA, 169
Confectionary food

Mars Canada Bolton, Ontario, 166, 167
Confectionary food

Matsushita Kotobuki Electronics (now part of
Panasonic) Vancouver, WA, 53
Electronics company

Mattel Canada Inc. Mississauga, Ontario, 181
Toy-manufacturing company

Media Kitchen, The New York, NY, 95
Global cloud-based media agency

MeetEdgar Austin, TX, 149
Social media scheduling platform

Meissner-Jacquet San Diego, CA, 121
Commercial real estate firm

Melbourne Manchester, England, 102
IT server hosting firm

Memorial Branch Library San Antonio, TX, 56
Library

Mendix Boston, MA, 126
App development firm

Meritor Troy, MI, 154
Supplier of commercial vehicle products

Merkle Inc. Burbank, CA, 88
Global performance marketing agency

Metis Communications Boston, MA, 141
Marketing and public relations firm

Microsoft Corporation Redmond, WA, 61, 200
Multinational technology company

Midtown Group Washington, DC, 161
Staffing and recruitment firm

Mission Support and Test Services North Las
Vegas, NV, 24
Nevada National Security Site

Momenta Pharmaceuticals Cambridge, MA, 98
Biotech for immune system disorders

Mood Media (aka Muzak) Austin, TX, 190
In-store music company

Motley Fool Alexandria, VA, 95
Private financial company

Moz Seattle, WA, 64
Marketing analytics software firm

Mutual Mobile Austin, TX, 181
Technology agency

MyEmployees Castle Hayne, NC, 123
Management consulting company

**Nationwide Mutual Insurance
Company** Columbus, OH, 110
Insurance and financial services

Nerdery, The Edina, MN, 101, 105, 165
Technology company

Netflix Los Gatos, CA, 141
Technology and media services

New York Times, The New York, NY, 96
American newspaper

NIC Inc. Olathe, KS, 65
Digital government service

Nicklaus Children's Hospital Miami, FL, 159
Hospital for children

Nitro Software Inc. San Francisco, CA, 194
Develops commercial software

North 6th Agency SoHo, New York, NY, 84
Brand communications agency

**Novartis Institutes for BioMedical
Research** Cambridge, MA, 97
Global pharmaceutical research

NowSecure Chicago, IL, 94
Software company

N2 Publishing Wilmington, NC, 184
Hyper-local magazines

Nugget Markets Woodland, CA, 59, 110
Grocery chain

Nutanix San Jose, CA, 188
Cloud computing company

OC Tanner Salt Lake City, UT, 121
Incentive company

OOPS! Co. Providence, RI, 187
Specialty store

Open Systems Technologies Grand Rapids, MI,
57, 100
Staffing solutions company

OppLoans Chicago, IL, 180
Online lender and service provider

Pacific Bell San Francisco, CA, 32
Telephone company

Pampered Chef Addison, IL, 180
E-commerce company

ParkWhiz Chicago, IL, 180
E-parking service

Patagonia Ventura, CA, 144
Adventure outfitter

Penguin Random House New York, NY, 122
Book publisher

People Business Solutions Inc. Wheaton, IL, 110, 140
Consulting company

Perkins Coie Seattle, WA, 134, 138, 174
Law firm

PetBox San Diego, CA, 167
Online retailer of pet products

Petco San Diego, CA, 168
Pet retailer

PetSmart Phoenix, AZ, 168
Pet superstores

Pinterest San Francisco, CA, 102
Social media service

Pixar Emeryville, CA, 63
Animation and entertainment studio

PLAE San Francisco, CA, 125
Custom children's footwear

Plum Organics Emeryville, CA, 57
Baby food manufacturer

Pocatello Police Department Pocatello, ID, 20, 33
Police department

Pocket Gems San Francisco, CA, 150
Mobile game publishing business

Policy Architects Toronto, Canada, 190
Life insurance agency

Poll Everywhere San Francisco, CA, 62
Collects live responses online

Pool Covers Inc. Fairfield, CA, 109
Pool coverings

Poppin New York, NY, 123
Office supply company

PricewaterhouseCoopers London, United Kingdom, 109
Professional services network

Prismier Bolingbrook, IL, 140
Contract manufacturer

Professionals in Human Resources Association (PIHRA) Los Angeles, CA, 27
Professional association

Profitero Dublin, Ireland, 195
E-commerce analytics platform

Progressive Insurance Mayfield, OH, 109, 152, 159
Car and home insurance

Promocodes.com Santa Monica, CA, 152
Coupon codes and deals websites

PTC University Boston, MA, 106
Education courses

PubMatic Redwood City, CA, 95
Programs advertisement

Pyramid Solutions Bingham Farms, MI, 100
Automation software

Qualcomm San Diego, CA, 175
Technology firm

Quantum Workplace Omaha, NE, 50
Employee engagement software

Quip San Francisco, CA, 179
Collaborate productivity software

Radio FLyer Chicago, IL, 185
Toy wagon manufacturer

Raytheon Waltham, MA, 140
Defense contractor and cybersecurity

Red Frog Events Chicago, IL, 153
Event production company

Red Sky Solutions Silicon Valley, CA, 176
Cyber security consulting firm

Red Velvet Events Austin, TX, 70
Creative planning agency

The Retina Group Washington, DC, 53
Ophthalmology practice

Retooling the Workforce Los Angeles, CA, 25
Online education firm

Reverb.com Chicago, IL, 173
Online marketplace for music gear

Riot Games West Los Angeles, CA, 109
Video game developer

Rover Seattle, WA, 166
Connector of dog owners with sitters and walkers

Salesforce San Francisco, CA, 199
Cloud-based software firm

San Diego County Bar Association San Diego, CA, 62
Legal community

SBC Global Chicago, IL, 44, 157, 169
Telecommunication services

Schmidt Harvey Consulting LLC Phoenix, AZ, 28
Coaching and consulting firm

Scripps Health San Diego, CA, 168
Nonprofit healthcare system

Scripps Memorial Hospital Encinitas, CA, 69
Hospital

SecureAuth Corporation Irvine, CA, 90
Global identity security firm

Sheetz Altoona, PA, 101
Convenience store chain

ShortStack Reno, NV, 165
Marketing software

Shutterstock New York, NY, 129
Stock photography business

Simple Truth Chicago, IL, 59
Brand development agency

SkinCeuticals New York, NY, 85, 122
Science-backed skincare

SkyeTeam Broomfield, CO, 134
Business management consulting

Smule San Francisco, CA, 172
Music app developer

SnackNation Culver City, CA, 71, 144, 200
Snack delivery company

Social Impact Architects Dallas, TX, 174
Social change agency

Southwest Airlines Dallas, TX, 185
Major American airline

SpaceX Hawthorne, CA, 176
Aerospace manufacturer

Sparks Philadelphia, PA, 121
Marketing agency

Spotify Stockholm, Sweden, 173
Music streaming and media services

Spyder Trap Minneapolis, MN, 165
Digital-only marketing firms

Square San Francisco, CA, 160
Financial service company

Standard, The New York, NY, 181
Boutique hotel chain

Standard Auto Parts Corporation Baltimore, MD, 69
Auto parts supplier

State Association of County Retirement Systems Sacramento, CA, 62
Retirement system

StumbleUpon San Francisco, CA, 162
Discovery and advertisement engine

Suburban Custom Awards & Framing Decatur, GA, 73
Custom award makers

Sunset Oakland, CA, 135
Magazine company

Sykes Tampa, FL, 144
Outsourcing provider

Synlogic Therapeutics Cambridge, MA, 83
Biotechnology company

Takezō Portland, OR, 47
Customized nutrition supplements

Tamayo Group Inc. Cardiff-by-the-Sea, CA, 62
Leadership and organizational performance

Target Corporation Minneapolis, MN, 114
Retail corporation

Team Building Covington, WA, 97
Creative activity provider

TechniGraphics Wooster, OH, 139
Engineering data company

Timberland Stratham, NH, 198
Outdoor apparel retailer

Time Warner Cable Milwaukee, WI, 63
Cable television company

TINYpulse Seattle, WA, 59, 160, 179
Employee engagement software

Toast Boston, MA, 189
Cloud-based restaurant software firm

Toister Performance Solutions Inc.
San Diego, CA, 22
Customer service training

Trader Joe's Monrovia, CA, 35, 136, 158
Grocery store chain

TransferWise Tampa, FL, 190
Money transfer system

Trello Software New York City, NY, 83
Web-based list-making application

Trial Runners Dickinson, ND, 156
Ophthalmology clinical research

TripAdvisor Needham, MA, 153, 195
Travel information company

Tripping.com San Francisco, CA, 61
Search engine for vacation rentals

Tripwire Portland, OR, 87
Software company

Trupanion Seattle, WA, 169
Pet insurance provider

Twice (now a part of eBay) San Jose, CA, 158
Online secondhand clothes company

Twitch San Francisco, CA, 152, 162
Gaming company

Twitter San Francisco, CA, 50, 72, 152
Microblogging and social networking

2Connect San Diego, CA, 90
Presentation coaching and training firm

Uber San Francisco, CA, 38, 114
Transportation company

Underscore Boston, MA, 97
Venture capital firm

United Way Alexandria, VA, 195
Nonprofit organization

University of Washington Seattle, WA, 188
Public university

UnleashedLeaders.com San Francisco, CA, 85, 102
Executive coaching

UPS Atlanta, GA, 77
Shipping giant

Utility Concierge Dallas, TX, 175
Connects utilities and home services

ViaSat Carlsbad, CA, 65
Broadband services and technology

VideoAmp Santa Monica, CA, 128, 195
Video advertising optimization

Vimly Benefits Solutions Mukilteo, WA, 161
Information systems consulting company

Virgin Group London, United Kingdom, 50, 59
Venture capital conglomerate

Vistage International San Diego, CA, 21
CEO peer mentoring

Vox Media New York, NY, 95
Digital media company

Vuka Solana Beach, CA, 50
Natural energy drink company

Walt Disney Company, The Burbank, CA, 72, 185
Mass media and entertainment

Walt Disney World Swan & Dolphin Resort Lake Buena Vista, FL, 49
Hotel resort

Warby Parker New York, NY, 77, 119, 196
Prescription glasses retailer

Wegman's Food Markets Rochester, NY, 156
Family-owned supermarket chain

Wellframe Boston, MA, 181
Provider of health management solutions

Williamson Group (Cowan Company) Brantford, Ontario, Canada, 161
Financial services company

WillowTree LLC Charlottesville, VA, 189
Software applications firm

Windy City Fieldhouse Chicago, IL, 87
Corporate event provider

Workday Pleasanton, CA, 189
Cloud-based HR and finance software provider

Worldwide Marketing and Sales Longs, SC, 126
Consulting service

Xerox Corporation Norwalk, CT, 94, 181
Print and digital document services

Yahoo Sunnyvale, CA, 159
Web services provider

YouEarnedIt Austin, TX, 100
Employee engagement software platform

Zapier San Francisco, CA, 91
App-connecting software

Zappos Las Vegas, NV, 77, 88, 137, 149, 161
Online clothing retailer

Zoho Chennai, India, 64
Software development company

Zoom Video Communications San Jose, CA, 71, 139, 189, 197
Video communications business

Zoosk San Francisco, CA, 166
Online dating service

Zynga San Francisco, CA, 162, 167
Game developer

About the Authors

Bob Nelson, Ph.D., is considered the leading authority on employee motivation, recognition, and engagement and is president of Nelson Motivation Inc., a management training and consulting company located in San Diego, California (www.drbobnelson.com) that specializes in helping organizations improve their management practices, programs, and systems.

He helped to found Recognition Professionals International, a professional association dedicated to promoting the exchange of employee recognition best practices, and is the creator of Employee Appreciation Day, which falls on the first Friday in March each year.

He has been named a Senior Fellow by The Conference Board, a Top 5 Global Management Guru by Global Gurus, a Top Thought Leader by the Best Practice Institute, and a Global Employee Engagement Influencer by EE Awards. He has worked with thousands of organizations, including 80 percent of the Fortune 500, and has conducted presentations on six continents. He previously worked closely with Dr. Ken Blanchard, co-author of *The One Minute Manager*, for 10 years and currently serves as a personal coach for Dr. Marshall Goldsmith, the #1-ranked executive coach in the world.

Dr. Bob has sold over five million books on management and motivation, including *1501 Ways to Reward Employees*, *1001 Ways to Energize Employees*, *The 1001 Rewards & Recognition Fieldbook*, *The Management Bible*, *Ubuntu!*, *Managing For Dummies*, *Recognizing &*

Engaging Employees For Dummies, and most recently, *1001 Ways to Engage Employees*. Dr. Nelson's books have been translated into over 30 languages.

Dr. Bob holds an MBA in organizational behavior from UC Berkeley and received his Ph.D. in management education with the late, great Dr. Peter F. Drucker ("The Father of Modern Management") at the Drucker Graduate Management School of Claremont Graduate University in suburban Los Angeles. He has taught at multiple colleges and universities, including for MBA students at the Rady School of Management at the University of California, San Diego.

Mario Tamayo has 30+ years of experience in training, human performance, and organization development and has been an advocate of promoting company cultures of enjoyable employment and recognition—demonstrating that "work made fun does, in fact, get done." He has successfully leveraged the skills he demonstrated in the sixth grade at St. Michael's Academy—that won him the Class Clown and Least Likely to Succeed monikers—to prove his teachers were somewhat in error.

Mario is a principal with Tamayo Group Inc. (www.tamayogroup .com), a Cardiff-by-the-Sea, California–based leadership consulting firm. He coaches, writes extensively, and speaks and leads workshops on management development, presentations skills, and personal and professional empowerment.

He has been responsible for several successful performance and product improvement initiatives for organizations, including Amylin Pharmaceuticals, The Anthony Robbins Companies, Broadcom, The Ken Blanchard Companies, Life Technologies, Mitchell, Nelson Motivation, Petco, ProSciento, and Viasat.

After earning a master's degree from San Diego State University, Mario established the first values-based awards process for General Dynamics in the early 1980s. At GD, he developed and implemented Fit to Lead, a broad-scoped executive development and coaching program. Simultaneously, he codeveloped and directed the corporate wellness program—consistently ranked in the Top 10 in America.

At The Ken Blanchard Companies, Mario served as a company ombudsperson and mediator—working closely with Ken as his company expert on ethics, values, and recognition. He also served as Brand Manager and as Director of Product Development, where his team developed 250+ leadership products, including *SLII, SLII DiSC, SLII MBTI, Building High-Performing Teams, Raving Fans, Legendary Service*, and *Gung Ho* product lines that are used by companies worldwide.